An Interactive Study of Philippians

TO LIVE IS CHRIST

Thomas and Sheila Jones

Books from Tom and Sheila Jones

9 to 5 and Spiritually Alive
Sheila Jones

Deep Convictions
Tom Jones

Finding Balance from the Inside Out
Sheila Jones

God's Perfect Plan for Imperfect People—Ephesians
Tom and Sheila Jones

In Search of a City
Tom Jones

Letters to New Disciples
Tom Jones

Mind Change
Tom and Sheila Jones

Mind Change Moments
Tom Jones

My Bucket of Sand
Sheila Jones

No One Like Him
Tom Jones

One Another
Tom Jones/Steve Brown

TO LIVE IS CHRIST
An Interactive Study of Philippians
Copyright © 2019 by Tom A. and Sheila Jones
ISBN: 978-1-948450-36-2

Previous edition published by DPI, copyright 1993.

Published by Illumination Publishers, 6010 Pinecreek Ridge Court, Spring, Texas 77379, (www.ipibooks.com).

Printed in the United States of America.

Illumination Publishers titles may be purchased in bulk for class-room instruction, business, fund-raising, or sales promotional use. For information, please e-mail paul at paul.ipibooks@me.com.

Illumination Publishers cares deeply about using renewable re-sources and uses recycled paper whenever possible.

Interior text layout and cover design by Toney C. Mulhollan.

About the authors: Tom Jones and his wife, Sheila, make their home in the Nashville area and serve with the Greater Nashville Church. Tom is the author of *No One Like Him: Jesus and His Message, The Baptized Life,* and many other books. Sheila's most recent book is *My Bucket of Sand.*

CONTENTS

PREFACE

A DIFFERENT APPROACH

Readers of the first four volumes of the Daily Power Series will quickly recognize that we have taken a different approach with this volume. First, the entire book deals with one New Testament letter—Paul's letter to the Philippians; and second, all the material here was written by the two of us, not by a larger group of authors. Because we realize readers have appreciated the previous diversity of authors, we do have plans to return to that format in future volumes.

We have taken a different approach in this volume for two reasons. First, we felt that more continuity could be maintained in working through one New Testament document if only two writers (married to each other!) were working with all the material. But second, and perhaps more important, we wanted to produce a book that would call on the reader to get more involved and spend more time with his or her own personal response. One of the most moving features of our earlier volumes has been the personal sharing combined with the writers' comments on the biblical text. In this volume, we will be asking *you*, the reader, to interact with the material so that *you provide the personal sharing*. We want to make sure we are continuing to apply the scriptures and the readings personally.

We have taken short sections of this powerful letter and attempted to give some comments that add insight to the text. Then comes the "Into Your Life" section where you think through and write down how you can apply the principles found in Philippians. In many ways, this book will be as good as you make it!

As you study, our prayer is that you will get to know at least three people far better than you know them now. First, you will be reading one of the warmest and most personal of all Paul's letters. Philippians gives you a unique opportunity to know the heart and mind of this dynamic, yet very human, leader whose work changed the lives of thousands. While you will get to know Paul through his writing, his primary concern would be that you get to know Jesus, the Christ. Paul would have been pleased with the title of this book: *To Live Is Christ!* He believed that to the core of his being. What he shares here, he shares in order that we might all know Christ and the power of his resurrection. Finally, it is our prayer that you will get to know yourself better, that you will be able to see how God has blessed you and changed you, as well as what still needs to be changed in your life.

You will know which of us wrote each article by the initial at the end. We will conclude the book by sharing in the epilogue how we have been personally impacted and changed by our study of Philippians.

One final suggestion: Close this book and take the time to read the entire letter to the Philippians at one sitting before you begin your study. Remember that it most likely would have been read aloud all at once to the church in that city. Put yourself in the place of the disciples who first heard it. Pray for God to bring its message ringing down through the centuries so that you will learn afresh that *to live is Christ!*

Thomas and Sheila Jones
Series Editors

PAUL HAD LEARNED THAT FULLNESS OF LIFE IS NOT DETERMINED BY CIRCUMSTANCES, BUT BY THE GOD YOU KNOW AND BY HOW DEEPLY YOU UNDERSTAND HIS LOVE.

1

THE MAN KNEW
HOW TO LIVE

God is always surprising us. Who would have expected him to use a short letter written by a prisoner in first-century Rome to a church in a small, uncelebrated city to teach millions of people the true keys to life and happiness? But then, who expected him to teach us the power of love at the foot of a cross?

Sometime in the seventh decade of the first century A.D., chains were fastened onto a middle-aged Jewish man, whose appearance probably impressed no one, as he was held prisoner by the greatest power on earth. Later, with chains in place, he penned several letters to Christian churches around the Roman Empire. None of these letters showed any sign of despondency or discouragement, but one in particular, the letter to the church in Philippi, literally resounded with joy.

Victor Frankl, the psychiatrist and Nazi prison camp survivor, would write 1900 years later about the power that a deep sense of meaning can give to a person even in the worst circumstances. His first-century Jewish brother Paul understood this long before the advent of modern psychology. He had lived a hard life. He had been accused, persecuted, beaten, banished and then arrested and imprisoned; but through it all, the man showed that he had learned how to live. He had learned that fullness of life is not determined by circumstances, but by the God you know and by how deeply you understand his love.

As he writes to the church in Philippi, he stands falsely charged by the governing powers. Among religious people there are those who are trying to undermine his authority and compete with him for influence. Even some of his own brothers in the faith are acting with insincerity. Sisters in the faith are behaving contentiously with one another. In all likelihood, he has not seen some of his own dreams come true—like taking the message about Jesus Christ all the way to Spain. But no matter—the man is grateful. He could list for you 100 things that had not gone well. But he is still thankful and joyful. What does he know that we need to know?

Helping others find his powerful secret is what this little book is all about. Take a piece of this letter to the Philippians each day for the next month and consider it carefully, and you too can find what Paul had found. He says he "learned" it (Philippians 4:12). It took him some years to learn it. At one point in his life, even as a disciple, he did not yet understand all that he shares in this letter. The secret doesn't just fall from the sky and land somewhere in our heads. We don't catch it as one catches a virus, though it certainly helps to be around people who know it. The way you get the secret into your head and into your heart is to do it the old fashioned way—to "learn" it. The first step is to learn it from what you read, and the second is to then *really* learn it by *doing* what you read.

Spend a month with Philippians and you will be ready for a lifetime of challenge. Spend 30 days with this ancient letter, and you'll be ready for good days and tough days, for encouraging days and disappointing days, for days of great pleasure and days of great pain. Take the message here and put it into your heart, and you will become a person of impact who shines like a star in the universe. Once you learn that "to live is Christ and to die is gain," there is nothing that can take from you that deep sense of joy.

Let God surprise you. Study this short letter written to people you've never met, living in a city you can't find on any map today, and discover how to live…whatever comes your way. Discover how to make a difference in a dark world, whatever your circumstances. ∎

INTO
YOUR
LIFE

What do you most want to learn about how to live?

What development in life would most challenge your ability to enjoy life? Why?

What are some of your greatest fears?

How has God already surprised you?

How many times have you studied this letter to the Philippians? What do you believe you can gain from a fresh study?

To LEARN TO LIVE IS TO LEARN TO DEEPLY CONNECT WITH OTHERS, AND NOTH-ING — ABSOLUTELY NOTHING — BRINGS PEOPLE TOGETHER LIKE THE GOSPEL.

2

PARTNERS IN THE GOSPEL

Paul and Timothy, servants of Christ Jesus, To all the saints in Christ Jesus at Philippi, together with the overseers and deacons: Grace and peace to you from God our Father and the Lord Jesus Christ. I thank my God every time I remember you. In all my prayers for all of you, I always pray with joy because of your partnership in the gospel from the first day until now, being confident of this, that he who began a good work in you will carry it on to completion until the day of Christ Jesus (Philippians 1:1-6).

Imprisoned and in chains, Paul's contact with others was severely limited. The man who had made a career of being with others and influencing their lives now saw only a few other human beings each week—his guards and the occasional visitors he would have been allowed. Was he overwhelmed with frustration? Feeling he had a right to be discouraged? Mired in depression? Not at this point in his life. Through many hard times he had learned to overcome the most challenging of circumstances. He had learned that the mind controlled by the Spirit is powerful and can break free of prison walls. It can take us to those who have shared their lives with us, even though they may be out of sight and hundreds of miles away.

Paul could remember the first time he ever set foot in Philippi. He could remember that vision of the man from Macedonia that led him on to the European continent. He could remember the first converts—Lydia and her household, the jailer and his household, and then others who followed. He could remember how, from another cold cell, God pulled one of his surprise attacks and used an earthquake to bring unlikely people into the kingdom of God (Acts 16:22-29). And most of all he could remember the church—the dear friends—that grew out of those experiences.

Philippi, named for Philip of Macedon (the father of Alexander the Great), was a Roman military colony and, as such, a city with fierce loyalty to the empire. It was not exactly a place one would expect the message of Jesus to take hold quickly—the official Roman report on Jesus was that he was crucified as a dangerous insurgent. When Paul and Silas ended up in the Philippian jail that was just where you would have expected them to be.

Precious Memories

But Paul's memories were not so much of his arrest and his harsh treatment. His memories were of God working to change lives through all those experiences. And as he sat in confinement in Rome, his mind transported him into the fellowship of Philippian disciples—now more than 1000 nautical miles and many hours away. Barely five lines into his letter we find Paul rejoicing. About what? The relationships God had given him with other disciples.

Christianity is most certainly a personal experience but, contrary to much modern thinking, it is just as certainly not a private experience. To learn to live is to learn to deeply connect with others, and nothing—absolutely nothing—brings people together like the gospel. First of all, disciples are joint heirs with Christ, sharing together in the amazing and lavish grace of God. Then we are colleagues, coworkers and fellow soldiers in a great common cause: the mission of taking God's grace to every person on the face of the earth.

But this must be more than a partnership on paper. It must be a partnership in practice. Paul could feel this way about the disciples in Philippi because they had worked together, prayed together, suffered together, and celebrated the victories together. Only when we have been in the trenches with others will we have relationships that are full of life. ∎

INTO YOUR LIFE

What experiences of yours have taught you the meaning of "partnership"?

How does prayer tighten your partnership in the gospel with other disciples?

What can you accomplish in "partnership" that you could never accomplish alone?

List the people you want to work with more closely in spreading the gospel, and put down one word or two that describes the commitment you want to make to them.

PERSONAL DECISION:

PAUL BEGAN A FAMILY AND CONTINUED TO HAVE THEM IN HIS HEART, TO NURTURE THEM AS THEY GREW TO BE LIKE JESUS. HE DID NOT ALLOW PAIN, DISTRACTION, NEW CONVERTS OR PROBLEMS TO LESSEN HIS COMMITMENT TO THOSE HE LEFT BEHIND.

3

I HAVE YOU IN MY HEART

It is right for me to feel this way about all of you, since I have you in my heart; for whether I am in chains or defending and confirming the gospel, all of you share in God's grace with me. God can testify how I long for all of you with the affection of Christ Jesus (Philippians 1:7-9).

We can know that Saul the Pharisee did not receive training in the rabbinic school to say, "I have you in my heart" or "I long for you with the affection of Christ Jesus." To the contrary, he would have been taught rabbinic logic. He would have learned how to tackle issues of the law, not how to hug and cry with people and cause them to feel loved.

This man was profoundly changed on his way to Damascus that day (Acts 9). During three days of blindness, intensive prayer and evaluation, his pharisaic crust had broken. His independence had melted as he regained his sight through the touch of another person—one of the Christians he had come to arrest. He recognized and embraced the true Lord of his life. Then, what else could a strong-willed, highly motivated person do except give everything he had to spread the truth he had found?

The Philippian disciples were profoundly impacted by Paul's change. From the first day, he had them in his heart, and that had changed their lives. A well-to-do business woman, servants and slaves from her household, a tough Roman jailer and his wife and believing children formed part of the nucleus of the church—people very different from each other. They were people who felt loved by God and by Paul—and they were learning to love each other, to have each other in their hearts.

Tenderness and Affection

This text is one of the most intimate and touching paragraphs written by Paul in his New Testament letters. When he prayed, the faces of the Philippian disciples came to his mind—their needs, their struggles and victories. In order to speak with such tenderness and affection, Paul had to have come to know them all. He was deeply committed to these brothers and sisters. He did not start a church and then move on to "bigger and better things." He began a family and continued to have them in his heart, to nurture them as they grew to be like Jesus. He did not allow pain, distraction, new converts or problems to lessen his commitment to those he left behind. As his letter was read aloud, the disciples must have felt secure in his love and encouraged in his trials.

Did some of the disciples have harsh, unbelieving husbands? He was committed to them. Did some have a physical challenge? He was committed to them. Were some getting along in years? Were some teenagers? Were some widows or parents of small children? He was committed to all of them. He had each of them tucked into a special fold of his heart. He was a leader after the spirit of his leader and Lord—he was a true shepherd of his people: "He calls his own sheep by name" (John 10:3). "The good shepherd lays down his life for the sheep" (John 10:11). "I know my sheep and my sheep know me..." (John 10:14). Saul the Pharisee had become Paul the shepherd, who carried his flock in his heart. He had learned to become compassionate and to express his emotions to people. He had learned to become vulnerable and to meet their deepest needs.

From persecutor to nurturer, he led the way for all of us to follow. No matter our background, no matter our personality, we too can long for people with the affection of Christ Jesus. To be like Jesus and Paul, we *must* have people in our hearts. ◖

INTO
YOUR
LIFE

Write down the names of five people that you consistently "have in your heart." Why is it so important to have specific people?

Write down the name of someone who is a role model for you in doing what Paul did with people. How does this person affect you? How do you want to imitate him or her?

How are you willing to be vulnerable in order to meet the deepest needs of others?

What most gets in the way of your having others in your heart? What can you do about these things?

PERSONAL DECISION:

Those who are satisfied with the love they have attained have really ceased to love.

4

TO LOVE IS TO LIVE

And this is my prayer: that your love may abound more and more in knowledge and depth of insight, so that you may be able to discern what is best and may be pure and blameless until the day of Christ, filled with the fruit of righteousness that comes through Jesus Christ—to the glory and praise of God (Philippians 1:9-11).

There is nothing greater than love (1 Corinthians 13:13). If we don't know how to love, we don't know how to live. To live as Christ is to learn how to love. Zeal is always needed, and since often it is one of the first things to be lost, we must be careful to maintain it. But as important as zeal is, without love it is nothing (1 Corinthians 13:3). When Paul thought of the disciples at Philippi, he thought of men and women who knew how to love. He had seen their love for God, their love for fellow disciples and their love for the lost.

Paul understood love's amazing capacity for growth, and he prayed for his friends that their love might develop. Love at any stage is good, but love can mature. Love can deepen. Love can be enriched with more wisdom and more insight. Love at any stage can be good, but love that isn't growing will soon die. Those who are satisfied with the way they love and are seeking nothing more will soon find that they are no longer making a difference. Those who are satisfied with the love they have attained have really ceased to love.

The Philippians had learned how to love, but Paul prayed for their love to "abound more and more." If you have been a disciple 20 days or 20 years, you still have much to learn about love. "God is love" (1 John 4:8). Learning to love is learning to be like God, and who among us can say we have arrived? Our love needs to grow "in knowledge and depth of insight."

Love must be far more than sentimental feelings. To truly do the best for other people, we must grow in our knowledge of God, his will and his truth (which is perfectly designed for people's lives). We must gain insight into what people feel and think and what makes them act as they do. We can have an impact on people at any point in our lives when we love as best we know how, but love itself demands that we seek more wisdom, depth and discernment so that we can even more powerfully affect the lives of family, friends, strangers and, yes, *even enemies.*

Pure and Blameless

"Pure and blameless" is not something most of us would feel that we are. We understand that *in Christ* we are "without blemish and free from accusation" (Colossians 1:21-22), and for this we praise God. However, we understand that this speaks of Jesus' finished work on the cross rather than of our own flawless behavior. We know well our own sinful tendencies, and that, apart from Jesus Christ, we would have no right to stand before God. But while being pure and blameless in our actual practice may seem only a distant dream, it is a dream that disciples must pursue nonetheless. We must pray for ourselves and for each other what Paul prayed here for his friends: that we may be able to discern what is best and then have the moral and spiritual courage to do it.

If in our hearts we hunger and thirst for such purity and righteousness, we *will be filled.* Paul's words in verse 11 echo what Jesus said in the Beatitudes (Matthew 5:6). Both here and in Matthew "filled" is in the *passive voice.* It is God who does the filling. Our part is to seek, to ask, to pray and to desire. It is God who then works through his Spirit to put the fruit of righteousness into our lives. And, certainly, abounding love is at the forefront of such fruit (Galatians 5:22). ∎

INTO
YOUR
LIFE

What were some of the first lessons you learned about how to love others?

What are some of the more recent lessons you have learned about how to love?

In what ways is your love abounding more than it was a year ago or two years ago?

How do you personally respond to this statement: "If we don't know how to love, we don't know how to live"?

What does being "pure and blameless" have to do with love? How are you pursuing what Paul talks about here?

PERSONAL DECISION:

OFTEN, WHAT LOOKS TO US TO BE SOMETHING "NOT GOOD" TURNS OUT TO BE COMPLETELY THE OPPOSITE WHEN WOVEN BY GOD INTO A LARGER PATTERN.

5

FROM TRIALS TO TRIUMPH

*Now I want you to know, brothers, that what has happened
to me has really served to advance the gospel. As a result, it
has become clear throughout the whole palace guard and to
everyone else that I am in chains for Christ. Because of my
chains, most of the brothers in the Lord have been encouraged
to speak the word of God more courageously and fearlessly*
(Philippians 1:12-14).

The successful life is not a life free from difficulty, trial or
tragedy. It is one in which a person finds a way to turn all
those things into victories for God. As he was going about his
glorious mission of taking the gospel of Jesus Christ throughout the world, a terrible thing happened (or so it seemed to
many)—Paul was arrested and imprisoned. On hearing such
news, some probably lost heart. Some may have doubted the
faithfulness of God. Some may have wondered if the message
could now go to the whole world. Most likely there were those
who said such things as: "Oh, no!" "Surely not!" "What will
happen now?" "This is awful!"

But the man in the midst of the turmoil had learned how
to *live*, and that meant how to live triumphantly through trials.
All those things you see above—and more—had been said one
Friday afternoon years earlier outside of Jerusalem, but Paul
had learned that what looked so tragic was really being used
by God to right the wrong and bring men and women to him.
Now he saw the same God working in his life to take *whatever
happened* and use it to advance the gospel. In this letter he reas-
sures his friends that what looks so bad is being used to get the
gospel into places it would not otherwise have gone.

In an earlier letter he had told the Galatians that it was
because of an illness that he had been given the opportunity to

bring the gospel to them (Galatians 4:13). Now he wants the Philippians to know that his imprisonment in Rome has opened the door for him to make known the message to the "whole palace guard." This is most likely a reference to the Praetorian Guard—the private army of Caesar himself. As we will see later, the apparent result was that there came to be disciples in Caesar's household (Philippians 4:22). Often, what looks to us to be something "not good" turns out to be completely the opposite when woven by God into a larger pattern.

Another Benefit

The situation Paul was in not only gave him some unique opportunities, but it strengthened other disciples as well. As they saw him not giving in or giving up, it deepened their convictions. As they heard how he had not lost one ounce of zeal but was boldly sharing his faith even with the imperial powers of Rome, it emboldened them to share the message in their own situations.

"Oh, no!" should be banished from our speech. *Whatever happens*, God is at work. "What will happen to us now?" The answer: God will take whatever has occurred and he will use it for good in the lives of those who love him. Satan never throws anything at us that God cannot handle. When tempted to say, "This is awful," we need to reevaluate through the eyes of God, who brings triumph out of trials again and again.

As we make the journey of faith, we *will* know hardship and we *will* see it in the lives of others. Disciples will be the "victims" of accidents, illnesses, violence and mistreatment. As we take the gospel into more dangerous areas, some of us will suffer imprisonment or even death for our convictions. But because of the sovereign power of God, whatever happens can serve to advance the gospel when we are living by faith. ∎

INTO YOUR LIFE

At what times in your life have you been most tempted to say "Oh, no!" or "Why this, God?"

When have you known of "tragedies" that were turned into triumphs for God? Have you seen this happen to churches? To individuals?

Is there anything happening in your life right now that God can use even though it does not look good or feel good?

Who has impacted your life positively because of the way they faithfully met some difficult circumstances?

What do you most want to learn from such people?

PERSONAL DECISION:

Paul was secure in his position before God—a saved servant of Jesus Christ. He was not concerned that he would lose importance in God's sight as others clamored for the spotlight.

6

CHRIST IS PREACHED

It is true that some preach Christ out of envy and rivalry, but others out of good will. The latter do so in love, knowing that I am put here for the defense of the gospel. The former preach Christ out of selfish ambition, not sincerely, supposing that they can stir up trouble for me while I am in chains. But what does it matter? The important thing is that in every way, whether from false motives or true, Christ is preached. And because of this I rejoice (Philippians 1:15-18).

From generation to generation the human heart does not change. First century or 20th century, the temptations are the same. The sins are the same. The needs and desires are the same. Man, naturally speaking, craves recognition and acclaim. Even within the blood-bought kingdom of God, we face these temptations. In the hearts of each of us, when we are distracted and self-reliant, we battle the demon of selfish ambition.

We might ask, "How could these men preach truthfully about Jesus and want to hurt Paul in the process?" If that seems incredible to us and like something we would never do, we are forgetting our human tendency. We need to take personally Paul's admonition to the Jews: "… you are condemning yourself, because you who pass judgment do the same things" (Romans 2:1).

Selfish ambition blinds us to our desire to tear others down as we build ourselves up. It may be subtle. No one may notice our comment—one which should not have been made, but was made to cause us to look better, smarter or more spiritual than another.

No doubt, these men coveted the *importance* of Paul's position, but not the painful *consequences*. Since they were envious and competitive with this apostle of God, we can know they were arrogant and thought too highly of themselves. They were much more concerned about their own glorification than they were about God's. The Greek word translated "selfish ambition" denotes a "ladder-climbing" person in our vernacular, focused on making it to the top. And their own sin surely kept them from seeing anything wrong with stepping on God's *anointed* on the way up.

Paul's Perspective

Paul was secure in his position before God—a saved servant of Jesus Christ. He was not concerned that he would lose importance in God's sight as others clamored for the spotlight. He did not fear that he would miss out on a spiritual "promotion" because he was out of the mainstream of the church's activity. His Lord had taught him to trust the working of the Father. He knew that these men would either become convicted of their sinful motives and repent, or God would judge them and deal with their sin. Whatever his reasons, he did not, in this case, condemn or mark them as heretics to be avoided by the church. If they taught truth and people were believing and accepting truth, then the mission for which he was in chains was being carried out. Bottom line for Paul: "What does it matter?...Christ is preached."

Paul was like these wrongly motivated teachers in one way—he too was *driven*. But his drive was not for self-glory or self-advancement. It was for the glory of the One who had turned his life upside down, who had given him hope instead of hate, and love instead of legalism. He was driven to love and to forgive. Paul must have been tempted to feel and respond in a natural, sinful way—even Jesus was tempted in every way. But, sitting in a damp, cold-to-the-bone Roman prison, he chose daily to take up the cross of Jesus and to take on the heart of God. More than anything he wanted people to come to know the Jesus he had come to know, and he was determined not to allow any person or any sin to impede the progress of this good news. §

INTO
YOUR
LIFE

How might you allow someone else's sin to affect your own efforts to spread the good news?

Have you ever wanted the respect someone else was given? Were you tempted to point out the person's mistakes or flaws in order to gain respect for yourself?

How can you guard your heart against selfish ambition?

How has Christ been preached in a difficult circumstance in your life?

What aspect of Paul's response encourages you the most? How can you imitate him in this area?

PERSONAL DECISION:

He knew who he was because he knew whose he was. To live is Christ. That summed it up. Christ was his life.

7

TO LIVE IS CHRIST

Yes, and I will continue to rejoice, for I know that through your prayers and the help given by the Spirit of Jesus Christ, what has happened to me will turn out for my deliverance. I eagerly expect and hope that I will in no way be ashamed, but will have sufficient courage so that now as always Christ will be exalted in my body, whether by life or by death. For to me, to live is Christ and to die is gain (Philippians 1:18d-21).

What is missing in so many people's lives is a clear sense of identity and purpose. They don't know when to say "No" and when to say "Yes," or when to speak up and when to be quiet, because they don't know who they are or why they are here. Paul suffered from no such identity crisis. He knew who he was because he knew *whose* he was. *To live is Christ.* That summed it up. Christ was his life. He had a relationship with God because of Christ. He had purpose in his world because of Christ. He had an example to follow because of Christ. He knew how to love others because of Christ. He had a destiny that was secure and unshakable because of Christ.

If his life was spared and he lived longer in this world, *Amen!* He would have a definite reason for being here. It would give him more time to show the life of Christ, mature those who were his disciples, and tell others the good news. His life circumstances were not what was important, whether in prison or set free, whether in plenty or want. What was important was that in *any circumstance* he would still have dreams on his mind, fire in his soul and love in his heart because he belonged to Jesus Christ. If, on the other hand, the Romans should execute him, *Amen!* When you have decided that to live is Christ, you can be sure that to die is gain. On another occasion he put it this way:

So will it be with the resurrection of the dead. The body that is sown is perishable, it is raised imperishable; it is sown in dishonor, it is raised in glory; it is sown in weakness, it is raised in power (1 Corinthians 15:42-43).

Not Ashamed

Because Jesus Christ was Paul's whole life, he could continue to rejoice *whatever* happened. In one way or another, unfolding events would turn out for his deliverance. He might be delivered from prison; he might be delivered from this life with all its struggles; or he might stay in prison and just be delivered from loneliness and anxiety, *but he would be delivered*. "He has delivered us from such a deadly peril, and he will deliver us. On him we have set our hope that he will continue to deliver us..." (2 Corinthians 1:10). Because this is what Jesus Christ does without fail, Paul was determined never to be ashamed of him. He sought the prayers of others and the help of the Spirit so that he would make Christ known with courage, whether facing life or facing death.

What could be better than to know who you are and to have an unswerving commitment to someone greater than yourself? What could be better than to have a faith that would enable you to face life and death, angels and demons, the present and the future, unafraid because you know nothing can separate you from the love of God?

A world of superficial people, whose only principle often seems to be "What is in it for me?" cries out for men and women with convictions to live and die for. A world of anxious people who try losing themselves in drugs, alcohol and sensuality cries out for men and women with a calm certainty and robust faith who can say "If I live, praise the Lord! If I die, praise the Lord!" ∎

INTO
YOUR
LIFE

Suppose you are on trial for making Christ your whole life. What is the evidence to convict you of the charge?

What most competes with Christ for the top priority in your life, and what is your attitude toward it?

How do you personally respond to this thought: "If I live, *Amen*, I know why I'm here. If I die, *Amen*, I know where I'm going"?

How has Christ taught you to really *live*?

PERSONAL DECISION:

1T IS ONE THING JUST TO "STICK AROUND" WITH PEOPLE BECAUSE IT IS NOT YET TIME TO LEAVE. IT IS QUITE ANOTHER THING TO COMMIT YOUR TIME, ENERGY AND LIFE TO THEM.

8

FOR YOUR PROGRESS AND JOY

If I am to go on living in the body, this will mean fruitful labor for me. Yet what shall I choose? I do not know! I am torn between the two: I desire to depart and be with Christ, which is better by far; but it is more necessary for you that I remain in the body. Convinced of this, I know that I will remain, and I will continue with all of you for your progress and joy in the faith, so that through my being with you again your joy in Christ Jesus will overflow on account of me (Philippians 1:22-26).

Paul was torn. He wrestled with his future. There was great advantage in dying, for then he would go on to be with Christ. The spiritual adrenaline was pumping as he rounded the curve and anticipated the finish line, but at some point Paul became convinced that God was saying, "There are more laps yet to run." There was a larger issue—the well-being of those he loved and discipled. He truly wanted what would be best for other disciples and for the kingdom as a whole.

He rejoiced that he would be able to encourage the Philippian disciples whom he loved. He did not rejoice that he would not have to suffer death. Death would have brought him face-to-face with the One he had lived for and died for. On the other hand, life would have brought more pain, more trials, more responsibility, more opportunities to become unfaithful, to stumble before crossing the line. But if it was to be *life* instead of death for Paul, it would be life for others, not for himself.

When he realized that he had more laps to run, he did not coast on all the good he had already done. Instead, he determined to run with all his might. He would continue his exhausting schedule, his traveling, his teaching, his warning with tears, his late nights and early mornings. He realized that living in the body would mean "fruitful labor"—daily hard work that would help the disciples to grow in spiritual discernment in their relationships, to grow in integrity in their jobs, to grow in trusting God in their prayer lives. Paul did not hesitate to speak the truth to people, even though it took considerable focus and energy to do so. He longed for others to know Jesus the way he knew him, and he would pour himself out to see that happen. Until he crossed the finish line he would find his life in helping others to grow in their faith.

To Live Is to Give

Paul had no desire simply to *remain* with the disciples. He wanted to *continue* with them. The Greek word translated "continue" means "to wait beside a person to be ready to help and to help all the time."* It is one thing just to "stick around" with people because it is not yet time to leave. It is quite another thing to commit your time, energy and life to them. For Paul to live was Christ, to live was to give himself to others for their spiritual progress and their deep joy. Whatever the cost of their growth, he would pay it. Would it mean being patient with someone who was weak? He would pay the cost. Would some take advantage of his humility? He would pay the cost. Would he have to wade into sticky, uncomfortable issues as families were brought back together in Jesus? He would pay the cost.

Paul could pay the high cost of *continuing* with others for their growth because Jesus had paid the highest cost for him. The more he took on the heart of God, the more he found joy where God found it—in giving to others. And God shows no favoritism. The same Holy Spirit and the same inner fountain of joy experienced by Paul are still available to us as we commit ourselves to others for their progress and joy. 🔊

---

* William Barclay. *The Letters to the Philippians, Colossians, and Thessalonians* (Philadelphia: Westminster, 1959) 35.

INTO YOUR LIFE

Obviously it is God's will for you to be alive. How closely does your heart mirror Paul's heart as he said, "I will continue with you for your progress and joy"? Are you alive to encourage others?

What cost is God calling you to pay as you "continue" with someone for his or her spiritual growth? Are you willing to pay it?

How can you deepen your inner fountain of joy so that you have more to give to others?

How does God show you that he is committed to you for your progress and joy?

PERSONAL DECISION:

This life that is worthy of the gospel ... is not just a good moral life. It is even more than a life of courage and gratitude. It is a life in which we, as disciples, are united with each other.

9

WHATEVER HAPPENS, UNITY!

Whatever happens, conduct yourselves in a manner worthy of the gospel of Christ. Then, whether I come and see you or only hear about you in my absence, I will know that you stand firm in one spirit, contending as one man for the faith of the gospel without being frightened in any way by those who oppose you. This is a sign to them that they will be destroyed, but that you will be saved—and that by God. For it has been granted to you on behalf of Christ not only to believe on him, but also to suffer for him, since you are going through the same struggle you saw I had, and now hear that I still have (Philippians 1:27-30).

After talking about his own circumstances and sharing his faith and convictions, Paul now turns to address his brothers and sisters in Philippi. He has set an example for them. Now he calls them to follow it. That is true leadership. They, too, must learn to face all frustrations with faith. They, too, must learn to handle disappointments with determination.

But we must understand that this challenge was not just for them, but for us who live 19 centuries later. Whatever happens—*whatever life brings*—we can conduct ourselves in a manner worthy of the gospel of Christ. That is the amazing thing about the gospel. It fits and it works, whatever develops and whatever does not develop. That is why Jesus Christ is the key to living. You cannot find a situation where his message cannot be lived out powerfully. *Whatever happens...in a manner worthy of the gospel.* That must be the motto we live by.

The Gospel of Unity

Living a life worthy of the gospel is a great general principle, but Paul has a particular application of it in mind. This life that is worthy of the gospel and grows out of the gospel, has a particular character. It is not just a good moral life. It is even more than a life of courage and gratitude. *It is a life in which we, as disciples, are united with each other.* The way we live so as to fit with the reconciling gospel of Jesus is "to stand firm in one spirit" and be so united that we and our enemies will find us to be as "one man."

Such radical unity in the religious world is seldom expected or sought. It is even looked upon with suspicion. But Paul says it is the mark of those living out the gospel. Jesus died to bring us together, and when "all the believers were one in heart and mind" and when "no one claimed that any of his possessions was his own" (Acts 4:32), the unbelieving world was seeing the gospel lived out before their eyes. The "autonomous Christian," so popular in our time, was unknown to the biblical writers. Commitment to the fellowship was not some "accessory" for those willing to pay more. It was an absolute essential that grew straight out of what Jesus did on that cross, and most of what Paul is going to say in Philippians comes from his concern that we understand this lifestyle.

Do we get the message? *We cannot be living a life worthy of the gospel if we are not doing what it takes to build unity in the body of Christ.* If we ever think it would be easier and better just to go do our own thing and not to have to work so much on all these relationships, our thinking has just left Christ. Staying in the fellowship will mean suffering; it will mean painful times; it will mean extra work; it will mean carrying each other's burdens, but the world needs to see the kind of family and friendships that are produced by the gospel. The world needs to see men and women, marrieds and teens, all races and colors, rich and poor brought together as "one man."

When the body of Christ is working in unity—after the hard work has been done to maintain it—it is a beautiful thing to behold. It is the gospel of Jesus incarnate in our world, and it will draw people to him. ∎

INTO YOUR LIFE

What would change in your life right now if you adopted the attitude: "Whatever happens, I will conduct myself in a manner worthy of the gospel"?

Why does a "manner worthy of the gospel" always mean working in unity with other disciples?

What kinds of things must you be doing regularly to maintain the kind of unity that Paul describes here?

What is there in your character that has some fear of or resistance to unity?

What power have you personally seen in unity?

PERSONAL DECISION:

EVEN WHEN HE CORRECTS US, HIS COMPASSION AND TENDERNESS SPEAK OF A DEEP AGAPE LOVE. JESUS IS A FRIEND WHO IS ALWAYS WITH US, WHO NEVER WILL LEAVE US.

10

HAVING THE SAME LOVE

If you have any encouragement from being united with Christ, if any comfort from his love, if any fellowship with the Spirit, if any tenderness and compassion, then make my joy complete by being like-minded, having the same love, being one in spirit and purpose. Do nothing out of selfish ambition or vain conceit, but in humility consider others better than yourselves. Each of you should look not only to your own interests, but also to the interests of others (Philippians 2:1-4).

Paul uses words rich in meaning to describe each disciple's personal relationship with Jesus. Verse one ripples with warmth and confidence. The image is one of Jesus coming alongside each of us, walking with his arm around us and encouraging us by sharing all the promises he will fulfill in our lives. He comforts and consoles us, carrying the burdens of hurt, disappointment, exhaustion, grief and illness. He cares infinitely about what is happening to us. Intimate friendship, a "sharing in the common life" ("fellowship") characterizes our walk. Even when he corrects us, his compassion and tenderness speak of a deep *agape* love. Jesus is a friend who is always with us, who never will leave us.

Paul wanted the recipients of his letter to bask in the incredible love of Jesus and to be reminded of the blessings of their relationship with him. Then, with that backdrop firmly in place, he called them to complete his joy by "being like-minded, having the same love" for each other that Jesus had for each of them. It was this Jesus who had said, "By this all men will know that you are my disciples, if you love one another" (John 13:35).

Love As Jesus Loved

He wanted them to come alongside and support each other, to share all the promises that God would fulfill in their lives. His desire was for them to comfort and console each other when hard times or challenging days came. A fellowship or "sharing in the common life" was his heartfelt vision for them. To know what was happening in each others' lives—and to care. And here is the key: He appealed to them to be the one to *initiate* this kind of love. To love like Jesus is to love *first*. "We love because he first loved us" (1 John 4:19). God did not wait for us to initiate, and then get an attitude because we didn't. Did someone's needs not get met while he was sick? When he is well, he should initiate to meet the needs of those who are sick. Did no one send a note when she was hurting? She should send one to someone she knows is hurting. Was he rejoicing over a victory and everyone was too distracted by their own problems to rejoice with him? He should be in tune with the next rejoicing person he encounters. When she needed to talk about some deep things in her heart, was a sister superficial in her response? She should be acutely aware of going to the level of someone's heart need in the future.

This is not to say that in all of the above situations the person should not talk with his brothers and sisters and share his or her hurt feelings. We need to be honest so we can *all* learn to be more sensitive. But we must not be self-absorbed or demanding about our needs being met. As Paul says in verse one, disciples are constantly encouraged and comforted by Christ's love and presence.

It is not natural to love this way. Thankfully, though, Jesus does not ask of us something he did not do or something we cannot do. The issue is: Will we trust the message he lived and taught? Will we die to ourselves and be the kind of friend to others that he has been to us? Or will we watch out for ourselves and withdraw from others when they don't meet our needs? A "grabby" life brings no peace, only the need to grab for more. The abundant life comes as we imitate our Savior by letting go of ourselves and having the same love for others that he has for us. §

INTO
YOUR
LIFE

Do you allow Jesus to carry your burdens, or do you try to carry them yourself? How do we cast our burdens on him? Why does he want us to do so?

Paul had a close friendship with Jesus. What can you do this week to grow in your friendship with Jesus?

The Greek word for "fellowship" (*koinonia*) can be translated as "sharing in the common life." What does it mean for you to share in the common life with someone?

What changes do you need to make to become more of an initiator in your relationships? How can you deal with what holds you back?

How can you keep from getting self-focused when you feel your needs are not being met?

PERSONAL DECISION:

BEING A DISCIPLE MEANS LOOKING INTO JESUS' MIND AND SEEING HIS ATTITUDE, THEN STRIVING WITH ALL THAT IS WITHIN US TO HAVE THAT SAME MIND AND ATTITUDE.

11

JUST LIKE JESUS CHRIST

Your attitude should be the same as that of Christ Jesus:
Who, being in very nature God,
did not consider equality with God something to be grasped,
but made himself nothing,
taking the very nature of a servant,
being made in human likeness.
And being found in appearance as a man,
he humbled himself
and became obedient to death—
even death on a cross! (Philippians 2:5-8).

As a traveler in a land of rolling hills suddenly comes upon a great mountain peak, so the reader of Philippians is given little warning that he or she is about to come upon one of the Christological high points of Scripture. Unexpectedly, in the midst of the discussion of the importance of unity in the fellowship of disciples, Paul writes this powerful statement about "the mind that was in Christ Jesus" (the literal translation). Theologians have written volumes about this passage, but what is important for us to understand is that there is to be a continuity between the mind of Christ and what goes on in the minds and hearts of disciples who are part of his church. The nature of Jesus is not some esoteric theological issue to be discussed only by the spiritually elite. Who he is, is a tremendously practical and relevant issue for all of us seeking to get along with each other and work together to make a difference in this world. *The way to have unity is to be like Jesus.*

No passage Paul ever wrote more clearly states what is involved in being a disciple of Jesus. It means looking into Jesus' mind and seeing his attitude, then striving with all that is within us to have that same mind and attitude. No man should ever dare call himself a Christian unless this is his passion. No woman should presume to have God's grace unless she wants that grace to produce in her the heart that is described here. "To this you were called, because Christ suffered for you, leaving you an example, that you should follow in his steps" (1 Peter 2:21). "In this way, love is made complete among us so that we will have confidence on the day of judgment, because in this world we are like him" (1 John 4:17). Peter, John and Paul all preached the same message. To live is Christ. To live is to be like Christ. To live is to have in us this mind that was in Christ Jesus.

The Nature of a Servant

Volumes can be written about the nature and work of Jesus (John 21:25), but in this passage Paul is concerned about one thing above all others. *Jesus willingly became a servant.* He is, in his very nature or essence (*morphe*), God. But he did not consider his divinity something to grasp or to use for his benefit. Instead, the Greek literally says, "he emptied himself." He poured out his divinity for us. He gave up his rights and took on the responsibility to serve us, "taking the very nature of a servant." He was in his essence God, but he became in essence (*morphe* again) a servant (*doulos*, a bond servant, a slave). The language here lets us know Jesus was not just playing a role, he was showing us the depths of his heart. "The Son of Man came not to be served but to serve…" (Matthew 20:28).

For God to become a servant is amazing, but there is more. Once in that state he humbled himself even further, becoming obedient to death—"even death on a cross." *Even death on a cross.* Those words would have resounded in the hearts of the Philippian disciples. As those who had been granted Roman citizenship, no Philippian would ever have to die on a cross. Death on a cross was *the death of a slave*. But that is how far Jesus went to serve. We are called to be just like him. ∎

INTO
YOUR
LIFE

What motivates you to want to be like Jesus Christ?

You will never be asked to "step down" as far as he did. But in what ways do you need to stop "grasping" and "step down" into a state of servanthood?

How does the whole idea of "servanthood" strike you?

Is there any type of person you don't like to serve?

How will implementing this passage change the quality of fellowship you have with others?

PERSONAL DECISION:

GIVE UP FOR GOD, AND GAIN. LOSE FOR GOD AND FIND. BOW BEFORE GOD AND STAND…JESUS IS LIVING AND EXALTED PROOF THAT IN BOWING, WE WILL SURELY STAND TALL.

12

EVERY TONGUE CONFESS

Therefore God exalted him to the highest place
and gave him the name that is above every name,
that at the name of Jesus every knee should bow,
in heaven and on earth and under the earth,
and every tongue confess that Jesus Christ is Lord,
to the glory of God the Father (Philippians 2:9-11).

Jesus Christ is Lord. Everyone who has ever lived will one day say these four words. Alexander the Great. Julius Caesar. Attila the Hun. Adolph Hitler. Queen Elizabeth. All the presidents, prime ministers and dictators of all the nations. Your next door neighbor. Your grandmother. *Everyone.* Paul tells us that "every tongue will confess" the lordship of Jesus—some in joy, some in regret, some sooner, some later. Unfortunately for most, it will be later.

Had someone told Pilate or Herod that this would someday come to pass, they would have scoffed. Observing the seemingly pathetic figure who stood before each of them, they would have had no clue that all would one day bow before him. The one who had seemed a weakling and a fool will one day judge the world by his sovereign Word. He said:

"Whoever acknowledges me before men, I will also acknowledge him before my Father in heaven. But whoever disowns me before men, I will disown him before my Father in heaven" (Matthew 10:32-33).

"If anyone would come after me, he must deny himself and take up his cross and follow me" (Matthew 16:24).

"I am the way and the truth and the life. No one comes to the Father except through me" (John 14:6).

These are exclusive statements from the one and only Son of God, yet his heart toward people was anything but exclusive. In fact, he was so *inclusive* that he became a bond servant, a slave, in order to include us with his Father.

Lose Your Life and Find It

His life, death and resurrection serve as a powerful demonstration of the truth he taught: "Whoever wants to save his life will lose it, but whoever loses his life for me will find it" (Matthew 16:25). He became nothing and lost his reputation among those who assigned such things in this world. He died a humiliating, ignominious, painful death—the death of a criminal. In the most real way, he *lost* his life for God and his will. Then, in the most real way, his life was *saved* as he was raised from the dead and exalted to the highest place. What further proof is needed? Give up for God, and gain. Lose for God and find. Bow before God and stand. But bow *now*! Not when the whole world by default will confess his lordship. Bow when you naturally want to be selfish. Bow when you want to be first, when you want your own needs met, when you doubt God's love or even his existence. Bow and say "Yes" to real life—now and *then*. Jesus is living and exalted proof that in bowing, we will surely stand tall.

The life of Jesus reflected what he taught: "Whoever humbles himself like this child is the greatest in the kingdom of heaven" (Matthew 18:4). When we seek to serve, greatness has a way of finding us. Each disciple must decide, as Paul did, that he or she lives among others "for their sake" (1 Thessalonians 1:5). Denying self and focusing on others is the way to eternal greatness—a way opened up for us through Jesus, who is Lord. ⟁

INTO
YOUR
LIFE

How does it affect you to realize that everyone who has ever lived will confess that Jesus Christ is Lord? Think of someone you know who has not yet confessed Jesus as Lord. Now think of the difference in their confessing him "sooner" rather than "later."

Is there any way you are seeking to "find" your life? What would it mean to "lose" your life in this area?

Greatness comes through serving. In what other ways have you sought to be great? What was the result?

Try to imagine what it will be like for God to exalt you with Christ to the highest place. Consider Romans 8:17.

PERSONAL DECISION:

OUR RELATION-
SHIP WITH GOD
IS VERY MUCH TIED IN
WITH HOW WE TREAT
ONE ANOTHER, HOW
WE WORK TOGETHER,
AND HOW WE RE-
SPOND TO LEADERSHIP.

13

WORK OUT YOUR SALVATION

Therefore, my dear friends, as you have always obeyed — not only in my presence, but now much more in my absence — continue to work out your salvation with fear and trembling, for it is God who works in you to will and to act according to his good purpose (Philippians 2:12-13).

Are you wide awake? Ready for a new thought? How about this one: *Paul is not talking here about personal salvation.* Keeping this passage in the context that began in Philippians 1:27 makes it very possible that Paul is referring to the *corporate salvation* of the Philippian church. (Compare Revelation 2:4-5 where the corporate salvation of another church is definitely the issue.) "Work out *your* salvation" could very well be referring to "your collective life as a body of saved people." If they empty themselves for each other the way Jesus emptied himself (2:5-8), then the disciples will be as one, and they will contend with power and vigor against all who oppose them (1:27-28). On the other hand, if they serve themselves instead of one another, if they grasp for their rights and their privileges, there will be conflicts and dissension. The church will be as divided as the world, and just as lost.

Evangelical Protestantism, influenced by Western individualism, has a way of making everything seem to be an issue of *personal* salvation. In such an environment it is hard for us to read "salvation" and not think it is talking about whether "I" will be lost or "I" will be saved. But it seems more likely that Paul here is urging the church to make sure they are living out what God has put within them (namely such things as love, unselfishness, patience, kindness, grace and forgiveness). To show those things to one another and then to the world is to work out or "express" our *common* salvation. To fail to live by the Spirit, to bite and devour one another, to let wounds go unhealed, and to let walls stay between people, is to be as lost as everyone else.

"Fear and Trembling"

Traditional uses of this passage have basically communicated this idea: "Seek your own personal salvation with fear and trembling before God or else you could be lost." Other passages can certainly be used to make such a point, but here there is another possibility. Surprisingly, "fear and trembling" may refer to what needs to go on between disciples, not just what goes on between disciples and God. In 2 Corinthians 7:15, Paul describes the relationship of Titus to the Corinthian church: "And his affection for you is all the greater when he remembers that you were all obedient, receiving him *with fear and trembling*" (emphasis added). There was apparently in this affectionate relationship a healthy sense of respect and awe for the way God worked through people. There was *not* an attitude that said, "This is just a man, not God, so we don't have to be that careful or concerned." There was an understanding that our relationship with God is very much tied in with how we treat one another, how we work together and how we respond to leadership (see also 1 John 4:20).

If our thesis is correct, the message is: *Our relationships are sacred.* They are vital to the work of God. Treat them lightly, don't give them much attention, don't settle matters quickly, let conflicts fester, and Satan will soon have a group he will use against the kingdom of God, regardless of what name it wears. "Working out your salvation" is not just a matter of getting right with God. It is also a matter of getting right and staying right with each other.

"Live a life worthy of the calling." "Work out your salvation." Here in Philippians it seems most likely that we should understand both of these to be about the same thing—"being like-minded, having the same love, being one in spirit and purpose." As Jesus himself taught, this shows all men that truly, we are saved disciples of his (John 13:34-35). ∎

INTO
YOUR
LIFE

How do you feel about obeying leaders whom God has placed in your life? (See not only 2 Corinthians 7:15 referred to here but Hebrews 13:17 as well.) What does it reveal if we are resistant to this concept?

What do your present relationships show about the effect of the gospel in your life?

How can you demonstrate more reverence and awe for the relationships God has given you in the body of Christ? How do you need to approach these with more "fear and trembling"?

Why is it so important to keep in mind that "God is at work in you"? What difference is made when we think of "you" as "all of you *collectively*"?

What can you do today to make the fellowship of disciples more in accord with the will and "good purpose" of God?

PERSONAL DECISION:

We are not to shine just to look good or to impress others with the brightness of our lights. The purpose of being resplendent in our purity is to "hold out the word of life" to a world lost in the darkness.

14

SHINING LIKE STARS

Do everything without complaining and arguing, so that you may become blameless and pure, children of God without fault in a crooked and depraved generation, in which you shine like stars in the universe as you hold out the word of life—in order that I may boast on the day of Christ that I did not run or labor for nothing. But even if I am being poured out like a drink offering on the sacrifice and service coming from your faith, I am glad and rejoice with all of you. So you too should be glad and rejoice with me (Philippians 2:14-18).

The darker the night, the brighter the stars. Few sights are more breath-grabbing. The array of stars—both their order and their brilliance—commands our attention and admiration. These stars have the same mesmerizing effect now as they did two thousand years ago when Paul gazed at them half a world away. They are a testimony to the timelessness of God's plan—for stars *and* for people.

Dark nights were also as dark as they are now. Paul's generation was as "crooked and depraved" as is our own. We may have fewer societal restraints, but there is no real restraining of the sinful heart. People then had the same "What's-in-it-for-me?" attitudes as they do now: "I'm not going to do any more than I have to." "Why should I work? She isn't!" "I want to do *what* I want to do *when* I want to do it. I don't really care who it hurts. After all, my happiness is the most important consideration here." Lust, selfishness, pride, deceit—our century has no corner on the commodities of the sin market.

Against such a backdrop, true disciples of Jesus are as evident as stars on the darkest of nights. The expression of the sinful nature that Paul focused on eradicating in the lives of the Philippians was a complaining, murmuring, argumentative attitude. This is key. He called the disciples to do a heart check. The one writing from a Roman prison displayed no trace of such a negative response. If anyone might have been excused for complaining, murmuring or arguing, it would have been Paul. The fact that he doesn't, speaks a powerful message to us all—first century, 20th and 21st centuries.

When the weather is lousy and we don't complain; if someone insults us and we don't insult them in return; when our employer asks us to do a task we don't enjoy and we don't mutter under our breath as he walks away; as our teacher gives an assignment and we don't whine with the others, we shine like stars in a self-centered universe.

Why Shine?

We are not to shine just to look good or to impress others with the brightness of our lights. The purpose of being resplendent in our purity is to "hold out the word of life" to a world lost in the darkness. Just as the star of Bethlehem guided the wise men to Jesus, so our star, when combined with the truth we speak, will guide wise men and women to Jesus today. The difference in our lives, our sense of inner peace, our love for others, our lack of protection of ourselves will show people a new way, an abundant life—the one God intends for them to have also.

As Paul appeals to the Philippian church to be "one in spirit and purpose," he envisions a whole constellation of stars—not one or two widely spaced lights in the vast darkness of the expanding horizon. People may respond to our individual lives at first, but as they are exposed to the whole assembly of disciples, they will see the splendor of God's power. They will see weak and sinful people just like themselves who, by the grace of God, are "blameless" and "without fault." They will see people who are committed to unity of thought and mind, and who experience the security that only comes as a result of being at one with God and with others.

Let it shine! Let it shine! Let it shine! ◼

INTO YOUR LIFE

In what setting have you most clearly seen the "What's-in-it-for-me?" attitudes described in the second paragraph? In what ways did you shine in that darkness?

Stars are different from moons in that they do not *reflect* light, they *generate* it. In other words, we are personally responsible for our spiritual growth. How well are you taking on this responsibility?

In what situations are you tempted to complain and murmur? What decisions will you make to change?

In order to shine consistently, we must care about the effect our lives have on others. How aware are you of the way you affect others? How can you become more aware?

How unified are you with others in sharing your faith? Do you see yourself as only a single star or part of a larger constellation?

PERSONAL DECISION:

TIMOTHY WAS NOT MILDLY OR MODERATELY INTER-ESTED IN KINGDOM BUSINESS. HE WAS A PURPOSEFUL, SELFLESS AND DEDICATED SER-VANT OF JESUS CHRIST— A MAN SOLD OUT FOR THE CAUSE.

15

NO ONE ELSE LIKE HIM

I hope in the Lord Jesus to send Timothy to you soon, that I also may be cheered when I receive news about you. I have no one else like him, who takes a genuine interest in your welfare. For everyone looks out for his own interests, not those of Jesus Christ. But you know that Timothy has proved himself, because as a son with his father he has served with me in the work of the gospel. I hope, therefore, to send him as soon as I see how things go with me. And I am confident in the Lord that I myself will come soon (Philippians 2:19-24).

Sometimes the people who make the greatest impressions on others are not the ones we would have expected. A tough Roman centurion and a feisty Canaanite woman made great impressions on Jesus Christ (Matthew 8:5-10 and 15:21-28). A young disciple named Timothy, who struggled with frequent illness, and maybe a good deal of fear (1 Timothy 5:23; 2 Timothy 1:7), made a powerful impression on the Apostle Paul. Nothing we read in the NT indicates that Timothy was an impressive speaker or one with a charismatic personality; but he made an impression even on the "greats" because he looked out not for his own interests but for the interests of others and that of Jesus Christ. In short, he lived out the message we have been describing in this book. He knew what it meant to "go to the cross." He knew what it meant to be a servant. He was convinced that he was never more alive than when he was dead to the old self and living for Christ.

Timothy had "proved himself." His discipleship was not a matter of talk, but a matter of practice. Those who spent time with him would have had no trouble seeing that the mission of Jesus, the health of the church and the good of the kingdom were his priorities. He was not a soldier who got entangled in civilian affairs. He was not a runner who ran aimlessly. He was not a boxer beating the air. He was not mildly or moderately interested in kingdom business. He was a purposeful, selfless and dedicated servant of Jesus Christ—a man sold out for the cause.

Eager to Send Him

No wonder Paul said, "I hope to send him to you soon." Timothy was the kind of person you would want to send. He would be "a letter from Christ…written not with ink but with the Spirit of the living God, not on tablets of stone but on tablets of human hearts" (2 Corinthians 3:3). His presence could do nothing but good for the church. He was the kind of person God wants to set right in the middle of every group that wears Jesus' name. Those with whom he interacted would see more of Jesus and feel more of Jesus. He would have no interest in gaining recognition but great interest in growing the kingdom. He would be oblivious to his title or his position and preoccupied with the plans of God and the needs of others. Sure, someone might criticize him. There are those who find fault with the best of people. But criticism would not stop him, because he would have his eyes on Jesus Christ.

How do *Timothys* come about? They study to become like this. They pray to become like this. They are discipled and they imitate to become like this. They persevere to become like this. They do whatever it takes. And God, in turn, uses them to bless the world. ∎

INTO YOUR LIFE

If leaders were looking for ways to shore up a weak group, would they "hope to send you soon"? Why or why not?

How deeply do you believe that you can be such a person? How often do you pray that you will be such a person?

What would need to change for you to be more like Timothy?

Write down the names of some "ordinary" disciples you have known who, nevertheless, make a great impression on others. What can you learn from each one of these?

PERSONAL DECISION:

FIRST AND FORE-MOST, GREAT FRIENDS IN THE KINGDOM OF GOD ARE ALWAYS "BROTHERS" OR "SISTERS" IN CHRIST. THEY ARE FAMILY.

16

BROTHER, FELLOW WORKER AND FELLOW SOLDIER

But I think it necessary to send back to you Epaphroditus, my brother, fellow worker and fellow soldier, who is also your messenger, whom you sent to take care of my needs. For he longs for all of you and is distressed because you heard he was ill. Indeed he was ill, and almost died. But God had mercy on him, and not on him only but also on me, to spare me sorrow upon sorrow. Therefore I am all the more eager to send him, so that when you see him again you may be glad and I may have less anxiety. Welcome him in the Lord with great joy, and honor men like him, because he almost died for the work of Christ, risking his life to make up for the help you could not give me (Philippians 2:25-30).

What a refreshment Epaphroditus must have been to Paul! In an environment where some brothers were jealous and undermined his leadership, Epaphroditus was devoted to him. He even went as far as risking his life to meet Paul's needs.

This loyal friend played a multifaceted role in Paul's life. He described him as a "brother, fellow worker and fellow soldier." First and foremost, great friends in the kingdom of God are always "brothers" or "sisters" in Christ. They are *family*. Epaphroditus was committed to Paul in the most difficult of circumstances. Being a prisoner, among other obvious drawbacks, was just plain humiliating. Even the most mundane aspects of daily existence were demeaning. To have a dear brother to encourage you and not be ashamed of you during such times must have meant the world to Paul.

Great kingdom friends are also *fellow workers*. With them we share a common task, and we labor to accomplish common goals. Having a fellow worker who could understand and share his purpose would have encouraged Paul greatly. Any time we are in a lonely or hostile environment, the presence of a spiritual comrade builds our confidence and courage.

But then great friends in the Lord are also *fellow soldiers* in the Lord's army. There is a spiritual war going on. There is a common enemy and a common battle plan: "Go and make disciples." As "army buddies," Paul and Epaphroditus burned with the same passion to see the world won, to see people surrender their hearts to the Master of the plan. Brother, worker, soldier—we need all these relationships in our lives.

He Did Not Grasp

As much as he needed Epaphroditus, Paul wanted above all to do what would most encourage his faithful friend *and* his family in Philippi. Obviously, the tie of affection was strong between this messenger and his sending church. He longed for them, knowing they would be eager to see him amid reports of his being "near neighbor to death" (literal Greek).

How easy it is to get so wrapped up in our own needs that we make decisions considering only how the outcome will affect *us*. We fear that if we are selfless in our thinking, we will lose out in some way. If we had been in Paul's situation, we might have reasoned, "They have each other. I need Epaphroditus more than they do." But we see Paul's selfless attitude as he thought of the needs of others and trusted God to meet his own needs. We also see from his life that such faith is always rewarded.

Paul was *eager* to send Epaphroditus back home—not *reluctant*, not *begrudging*, not *resigned*. Dismissing any tendency on their part to feel guilty that he was left behind in prison, he encouraged the disciples to welcome Epaphroditus with joy. He was gracious in his loss and thankful for their gain. Paul was supremely grateful for the fellowship with disciples, but he never hinged his own faithfulness on their support or presence. With focus on others and not on himself, he looked to Jesus Christ for strength as he always had done. ▌

INTO
YOUR
LIFE

In what ways have other disciples refreshed you? Describe one person who has this effect on your life. Which of his or her personal qualities is the most outstanding?

Of the three aspects describing Paul's relationship with Epaphroditus, which is your strongest area and which is your weakest—brother/sister, fellow worker or fellow soldier? Ask those close to you how they see it and why.

When has a spiritual comrade encouraged you when you were in a lonely or hostile situation? Have you been grateful to them and to God?

Which close relationship have you had to "let go of" in some way (through breaking up, moving, death, etc.)? How did you handle the emotional hit? Did you allow the hurt to damage your faith or deepen it?

Certainly you need to be tight with your brothers and sisters as God intended, but sometimes you are unable to be in touch with another disciple. How does such a time test the closeness of your relationship with God? Think of such a time and how you responded. What did you learn about yourself?

PERSONAL DECISION:

THE GRACE MODEL IS REVOLUTIONARY. SOMETIMES IT SEEMS TOO EASY TO BE TRUE. FROM ANOTHER ANGLE, IT IS WAY TOO HARD FOR OUR EGOS TO ACCEPT.

17

NO CONFIDENCE IN THE FLESH

Finally, my brothers, rejoice in the Lord! It is no trouble for me to write the same things to you again, and it is a safeguard for you. Watch out for those dogs, those men who do evil, those mutilators of the flesh. For it is we who are the circumcision, we who worship by the Spirit of God, who glory in Christ Jesus, and who put no confidence in the flesh— though I myself have reasons for such confidence. If anyone else thinks he has reasons to put confidence in the flesh, I have more (Philippians 3:1-4).

Disciples of Jesus are a strange lot. They can at the same time rejoice like crazy *and* talk soberly about serious problems. They do not have to be free of difficulties to be rejoicing with gusto. Paul introduces this section of the letter with a call to rejoice *in the Lord*. There are plenty of challenges in life, especially for cross-bearing "maniacs," but no matter what happens, disciples are *in the Lord* and that overshadows everything else. We will see this principle again and again in the rest of this letter. Being with Jesus Christ gives one an unquenchable joy and justification for what looks to others like a case of being "unreasonably joyful."

The joy Paul describes comes from Jesus. The problem he describes comes from men who don't appreciate Jesus. He describes them as "dogs," as "men who do evil," as "mutilators of the flesh."

Calm down, Paul. They are only Judaizing zealots who think men must be circumcised to be saved. That may not be right, but is it all that bad?

"Calm down," may seem to be the wise and cool response, but the Spirit-led Paul understood something that many do not. There are two options in approaching God: (1) the *performance* model and (2) the *grace* model. Paul had tried them both. One works; the other is a disaster.

Man, in his pride, self-righteousness and self-confidence, is naturally drawn to the performance model. We want the list of requirements. We want to check them off. We want to feel righteous because of what we did. These "dogs" Paul refers to were people who knew about Jesus Christ and even acknowledged him as Lord, but just wouldn't let go of the performance model. In their case this involved holding on to certain Jewish regulations that had been fulfilled and made obsolete by Jesus. They kept these, expected others to do the same and accepted as brothers only those who followed suit. But there was more here than dotting the right religious "i" or crossing the right theological "t." Fundamentally, they were still clinging to a system of self-justification that led to pride and religious snobbery.

The grace model is revolutionary. Sometimes it seems too easy to be true. From another angle, it is way too hard for our egos to accept. But in either case, this is what the gospel is all about and is, in fact, the source of this "unreasonable joy" we have described. The grace model says we are accepted not on the basis of performance but on the basis of our faith in the performance of another, namely Jesus Christ. It says there are never enough requirements we could meet, never enough rituals we could experience, never enough rules we could keep. It says that although we will be obedient even to death, our only hope of salvation is the grace that comes through the work of another. The gospel of Jesus is the clear message that such a model is the only working model. Praise God!

While the gospel is good news, it most certainly does not teach that just anything and everything is "okay." One thing that is clearly not okay is the performance model and those who preach it. Believe in it, use it and judge others with it, and you will go to hell. That is why the rejoicing Paul could still get so upset. It isn't likely that we will run into any "Judaizers" today, but we will have "dog days" until the world ends. "Watch out" is still valid. ∎

INTO YOUR LIFE

What does the phrase "rejoice in the Lord" mean to you?

How have you tried to live by the "performance model"? How are you tempted to live by it still?

What does the "grace model" produce in you?

Do you view preachers of a performance model the same way Paul did? Why or why not?

Why must we "put no confidence in the flesh"?

PERSONAL DECISION:

ALL HIS "SELF" RIGHTEOUSNESS WAS MOVED FROM THE PROFIT SIDE OF THE LEDGER TO THE LOSS SIDE. IF ANYONE HAD A RIGHT TO GLORY IN THE FLESH, PAUL DID. BUT HE SAW CLEARLY THAT NO ONE HAS THAT RIGHT — NO, NOT ONE.

18

FROM PROFIT TO LOSS

If anyone else thinks he has reasons to put confidence in the flesh, I have more: circumcised on the eighth day, of the people of Israel, of the tribe of Benjamin, a Hebrew of Hebrews; in regard to the law, a Pharisee; as for zeal, persecuting the church; as for legalistic righteousness, faultless. But whatever was to my profit I now consider loss for the sake of Christ (Philippians 3:4b-7).

Paul is most certainly thinking here about the Judaizing teachers—those people who twist the gospel and return to a performance model for salvation. If they want to talk about "confidence in the flesh," he is ready to take them on. If anyone is qualified to comment on that position, it is Paul. He lived it as consistently as anyone. Whatever the Judaziers might want to claim as accomplishments under the law, Paul says, "I have more." Perhaps they could dismiss Peter, who in the words from the musical *UpsideDown*, "never was a good Jew anyway," but Paul's credentials were very different.

Out of context, these statements may sound boastful, but in context we see Paul using the events of his life to show just how empty all human achievement is before God apart from the work of Jesus Christ. Elite heritage does not lead to exaltation before God. Recognition does not equal righteousness. Fervor does not necessarily show faith. These things may win the approval of men, but like the writer of Hebrews says of the blood of bulls and goats, they have no power to take away sin.

Neither Heredity nor Hard Work
Paul lists seven reasons he could have "confidence in the flesh," if that were the path to God. Four of these are based on birth, and three are based on work. First, he was circumcised

on the eighth day. In other words, he was born into the most Jewish of families. As Ralph Martin puts it, "The proudest of claims is put first; he is a true-blooded Jew from the cradle, and nursed in the ancestral faith."*

Unlike some of his Judaizing critics, some of whom were circumcised as adults, Paul underwent the rite at the earliest point. He had been part of the covenant people—"the people of Israel"—from the beginning. But beyond this, he was "of the tribe of Benjamin," the most honored tribe of all, the home of the holy city and the temple itself. He was a "Hebrew of Hebrews," most likely a reference to those families which were careful to pass on the Hebrew and Aramaic languages to their children even when they were living in a foreign culture as Paul's family was.

Paul's pedigree was impeccable, but just as importantly, he had, as he says to the Galatians, advanced "in Judaism beyond many Jews of my own age and was extremely zealous for the traditions of my fathers" (Galatians 1:14). He had committed himself to that most rigorous of Jewish sects, had vigorously opposed the church when it appeared to be undermining the Jewish traditions, and had kept the religious requirements in what he and others thought was a "faultless" manner.

But then came the Damascus Road, and a moment of clarity. Three days later came his baptism into Christ and the decision to consider all that "profit" really as a "loss." Literally the Greek reads "the things that were *gains* to me, I counted *loss*." The verb is the perfect tense which signifies a past action with a present effect. He is still counting them a loss. In the bright light of the righteousness of Christ, Paul's assessment of his religious performance totally changed. All his "self" righteousness was moved from the profit side of the ledger to the loss side. If anyone had a right to glory in the flesh, Paul did. But he saw clearly that no one has that right—no, not one. ∎

---

* Ralph Martin, *The Epistle of Paul to the Philippians* (Grand Rapids: Wm. B. Eerdmans, 1959) 141.

INTO
YOUR
LIFE

Does anything in your experience help you relate to Paul in all his religious correctness?

Many of us were the exact opposite of the pre-Christian Paul, but why is it still important for us to understand his point in this passage?

In what ways might the children of present-day disciples have to deal with the issue of heritage? How can parents help their children keep their thinking straight and appreciate the grace of God?

Why did Paul have to get so radical? Why consider all his "gains" as "loss"? Why go so far? Why be so hard on himself? Is there a lesson here for you?

PERSONAL DECISION:

BEING A DISCIPLE OF JESUS ALWAYS INVOLVES OBEYING HIM AS LORD, BUT AT THE SAME TIME HAVING A CLEAR — AND HUMBLE — UNDERSTANDING THAT OBEDIENCE DOES NOT EARN HIS GRACE.

19

I CONSIDER THEM RUBBISH

What is more, I consider everything a loss compared to the surpassing greatness of knowing Christ Jesus my Lord, for whose sake I have lost all things. I consider them rubbish, that I may gain Christ and be found in him, not having a righteousness of my own that comes from the law, but that which is through faith in Christ—the righteousness that comes from God and is by faith (Philippians 3:8-9).

Paul considered everything a loss in comparison with being under the grace and the lordship of Jesus Christ. Not only would he give up his religious pedigree and his performance in the traditions of his fathers, but he would gladly count anything and everything, past or present, as a loss in order that he might have Christ. But we must be careful here, lest we misunderstand. A superficial reading might cause us to think Paul is saying: "I would give up anything in order to be a disciple. I would give up my car, my house, my career, even my family." This is a conviction that Paul, no doubt, had (or would have had if he had owned a car!), but that is not the primary meaning of this passage.

Included in the things he "counted as a loss" would be "everything," even his performance and work as a Christian, as a missionary and as an apostle. His point is that he would not come before God holding on to his own accomplishments and claiming some reward for the good that he had done. Instead he would give up *any claim* that such things could make him righteous before God, believing that justification is by grace and not by works.

'I Consider Them Rubbish'

Referring to any personal accomplishments (either before or after his baptism), including many things that might have earned him recognition by men, Paul says, "I consider them rubbish." The word here (*skubala*) can either refer to human waste (the KJV translates it as "dung") or to food ready to be thrown on the garbage heap (what some of our grandparents might have called "slop" that they threw to the pigs). Paul is still reacting in this passage to those people who would teach the "performance model" (back in verses 1-3), and in the most vivid (some would say *gross*) way possible, he is telling us the same thing Isaiah did when he said that "all our righteous acts are like filthy rags" (Isaiah 64:6).

Certainly the good that Paul did by the grace of God was not dung or slop. But if he had seen *himself* as somehow the *source* of that good, had trusted in those acts of goodness, and had expected them to vindicate him, they would have been no better than dung when he stood before the judgment seat of God. This he clearly understood.

Being a disciple of Jesus always involves obeying him as Lord, but at the same time having a clear—and humble—understanding that obedience does not earn his grace. Our obedience—which is always imperfect—does not make us right with God. Instead, what accomplishes this is only "the righteousness...which is through faith in Christ—the righteousness that comes from God and is by faith." Some of us have a way to go in understanding this, and even those who do understand it can easily wander from it.

The message of the cross calls us to sacrifice everything to Jesus Christ, who has sacrificed everything for us. This we must do. No other response is right. It cannot be compromised. But here is the radical message of this passage: Once we have done that, we must glory not in our own sacrifice, but *totally* in his. Without his, ours would be worthless to God and to man. ∎

INTO YOUR LIFE

What good have you done since becoming a disciple? Do you trust in your own goodness or accomplishments? Do you think that those things will make you acceptable to God?

When are some times that you subtly slip into this way of thinking?

Why do you think Paul had such a radical view of performance and accomplishments? Why did he use such strong language to contrast what *we* do with what *Christ* has done for us?

How can you live a sacrificial life, one that involves denying yourself and taking up the cross, without taking pride in or glorying in your sacrifice? What keeps your head straight in this?

Why is Paul's message here "good news"?

PERSONAL DECISION:

BEING A DISCIPLE MEANS YOU WANT TO GROW IN YOUR UNDERSTANDING OF THE HEART AND MIND OF YOUR LORD. YOU WANT TO FEEL WHAT JESUS FEELS, TO HURT WHEN JESUS HURTS, TO BE HAPPY WHEN JESUS IS HAPPY. YOU WANT A CLOSE RELATIONSHIP WITH THE CHRIST—A DAILY, DEEPENING FRIENDSHIP.

20

TO KNOW CHRIST

I want to know Christ and the power of his resurrection and the fellowship of sharing in his sufferings, becoming like him in his death, and so somehow, to attain to the resurrection from the dead (Philippians 3:10-11).

I want to know Christ. The man who had a face-to-face encounter with the risen Lord said simply, "I want to know Christ." Did he not already know him? After three days of fasting and prayer (Acts 9:9)? After three years of personal training (Galatians 1:11-24)? After a visit to the third heaven (visions and revelations, 2 Corinthians 12:1-6)? Paul uses the Greek verb *ginoskein* which is kin to the Hebrew word that describes the sexual intimacy of marriage: "Adam knew his wife Eve, and she conceived and bore Cain..." (Genesis 4:1 KJV). The NIV translates the meaning of the verb, "Adam lay with his wife Eve..." Paul is not thinking sexually here, but he did want an ever-growing, personal, intimate relationship with Jesus Christ.

Paul knew much *about* Jesus. He wrote treatises about his supremacy and his sacrifice. But what was most important to this converted Pharisee was that he personally *know* this Jesus. Being a disciple means you want to grow in your understanding of the heart and mind of your Lord. You want to feel what Jesus feels, to hurt when Jesus hurts, to be happy when Jesus is happy. You want a close relationship with the Christ—a daily, deepening friendship.

In his obedience, Paul was well aware that simply doing all the right things would not give him intimacy with his Lord. He had tried that route, and it was a dead end. Christianity was not simply an upgrade of his pharisaic Judaism. Paul did not go from one form of legalism to another. He went heart-to-heart with God through Jesus, the only road with no dead end. And, through grace, he longed to share in Jesus' resurrection from the dead—to fully know the one who fully knew him.

Count the Cost

As disciples, we must daily count the cost. Do we really want to *know* Christ? To be a best friend to the Son of God? To share in all aspects of his life? Or do we simply want to be a name dropper? "Yes, I know Jesus Christ, the Son of God." Paul realized that to have an intimate relationship with Jesus meant dying to himself, "becoming like him in his death." There are no shortcuts, no scenic bypasses. The road leads to a cross—every time!

To become like him in his death is to become like him in his life. It is to give when you are tired. To pray when you don't feel like it. To stand your ground against powerful thoughts and emotions. To overcome fear and to love in practical, unselfish ways. To live like this is to know Christ. No wonder Paul also wanted to know the "power of his resurrection." He knew he could not live this way on his own. Neither can we. None of us can tame the unruly human heart. It must be changed and directed by the power of God himself. A lesser power is impotent to bring about change. Paul reminded the Romans that the "Spirit of him who raised Jesus from the dead is living in you" (Romans 8:11). The next time you look at what is being asked of you in a difficult relationship or a trying circumstance and you think, *There is no way I can do this*, remember that the power that raised Jesus from the dead lives in you as a disciple! The key to tapping in to that power is a desperate desire to know it and to know the One who gives it. 🔥

INTO YOUR LIFE

Do you ever try to substitute knowing *about* Jesus for actually *knowing* Jesus? How do you guard against a head-knowledge relationship?

When you look at Paul's life, how can you know that he always wanted to go deeper in his relationship with Jesus? Do you see that same desire in your life? How would others know that you had such a desire?

Is there anything in your life right now that calls you to count the cost of knowing Christ? Hurt feelings that need to be resolved? Disappointment over something that did not work out the way you had expected? A sin you need to repent of? The need to be humble and admit you need help? Whatever is happening, do you desperately want the power to respond as Jesus would have responded?

What does it personally mean to you that, as a disciple, the "Spirit of him who raised Jesus from the dead is living in you"?

PERSONAL DECISION:

SALVATION IS NOT THROUGH A "RIGHTEOUSNESS OF OUR OWN." BUT IF THAT THOUGHT LEADS TO SLOTH OR LAZINESS, WE SHOW WE HAVE MISSED THE GRACE OF GOD.

21

I PRESS ON

Not that I have already obtained all this, or have already been made perfect, but I press on to take hold of that for which Christ Jesus took hold of me. Brothers, I do not consider myself yet to have taken hold of it. But one thing I do: For- getting what is behind and straining toward what is ahead, I press on toward the goal to win the prize for which God has called me heavenward in Christ Jesus. All of us who are mature should take such a view of things. And if on some point you think differently, that too God will make clear to you. Only let us live up to what we have already attained (Philippians 3:12-16).

Salvation is not through a "righteousness of our own." But if that thought leads to sloth or laziness, we show we have missed the grace of God. There is so much more to know. There is so much more growing to do. The heart that understands Christ is "compelled by the love of Christ." The disciple who realizes that Jesus has taken hold of him wants to take hold of everything that Jesus has planned for his life. Such a one does not sit and wait for life to come to him; he "presses on." This word (*dioko*) was used in both hunting and foot racing. It could describe pursuing, chasing, even overtaking and capturing. Inspired by Christ, the true disciple wants to "go for it"—to discover all God has in the storehouses of his love.

A Time to Forget

There is certainly a time to remember (2 Thessalonians 2:5; 2 Timothy 2:8; Hebrews 10:32), but there is also a time to forget. If there is any tendency for us to "rest on our laurels," it is time to do some forgetting. If there is an inclination to get comfortable with what we have done, it is time to forget. Paul is describing a deliberate act of the will in which we decide not to cling to past accomplishments and past victories, but resolve, instead, to "strain" forward like a runner exerting all his energy to attain a new goal.

Paul, at the time of this writing, may very well have done more than any disciple of Jesus—living or dead—to advance the cause of the gospel throughout the world. The churches he had planted, the converts he had won, not to mention the abuse he had taken for the cross (see 2 Corinthians 11:24-28), could not be rivaled. But, remarkably, he did not cling to that. He purposely "forgot" it. (How can we doubt that the gospel radically changes people?) After all he had done, Paul did not consider himself one to have arrived. He did not see himself as the perfect disciple but as the transgressor still needing to be transformed. Since he was forgetting what is behind, he was as eager as a new Christian to find the next thing God had in store for him.

But surely Paul is a rare exception and surely God would not expect to find such an attitude in us all. Right? Wrong! All of us who are mature, Paul says, should think in the same way. It is the logical extension of the decision we made at some point in the past to deny ourselves, take up the cross and follow Jesus. Anytime we think: *Surely I've done enough; Surely, it is time for someone else to "go for it" for a while; Surely, God believes in retirement,* we are putting down the cross and taking up the cause of "self." With such an attitude, one has to wonder why we did "all the good things" that we now want to rest on. Was it so they would be *credited to us* or was it because we were in love with someone who had done for us what we never could have deserved?

Finally, Paul says let us live up to what we have attained. The way to take it higher is to hold on to what you have already grasped and then reach for more. ∎

INTO
YOUR
LIFE

What do you still want to learn?

Which of these phrases best describe your attitude toward spiritual growth?
a. relaxed coasting b. moderate walking c. focused running

Are you as eager as a new Christian to find out what God has in store for you next?

Ask someone who knows you well, who is honest, who loves you, and who is spiritually mature this question: Do I seem like a person who "goes for it" spiritually? Write down his or her name and a time when you will pop the question.

Why will the person with Paul's attitude have more joy than the person longing for "spiritual retirement"?

PERSONAL DECISION:

THE CROSS ITSELF STANDS AS A CONSTANT REMINDER OF THE BATTLE BETWEEN LIGHT AND DARKNESS.

22

ENEMIES OF THE CROSS

Join with others in following my example, brothers, and take note of those who live according to the pattern we gave you. For, as I have often told you before and now say again even with tears, many live as enemies of the cross of Christ. Their destiny is destruction, their god is their stomach, and their glory is in their shame. Their mind is on earthly things. But our citizenship is in heaven. And we eagerly await a Savior from there, the Lord Jesus Christ, who, by the power that enables him to bring everything under his control, will transform our lowly bodies so that they will be like his glorious body (Philippians 3:17-21).

Paul shows us by his life that the person who understands grace doesn't become a spiritual couch potato. A disciple "presses on." A disciple "goes for it"! Paul points out why it is so important that every Christian follow this example and live according to this pattern: *"Many live as enemies of the cross."* The acceptance of Jesus leads to joy but not to naiveté. Disciples are thankful, but still have their eyes wide open. This world is not full of sweetness and light. While it brings good news into our lives, the cross itself stands as a constant reminder of the battle between light and darkness. Jesus did not read a poem at Golgotha or offer some incense accompanied by a saccharine prayer. *He died there* because he had enemies. And now enemies abound who try to undermine what he did there. This is why it is so important for people like us to "go for it," to live according to the pattern, to resolve to know Christ and make him our lives. The war still goes on.

In Either Case

Some scholars think the "enemies" referred to are the Judaizing teachers to whom Paul has been responding in this chapter. Others think he may be referring to antinomian teachers in the church who relaxed morality and gave license to sensual indulgence (like those in 2 Peter 2:17-22). A strong case could be made for either, and the truth is that both extremes are opposed to the cross of Christ. To act as though we could do enough to earn our salvation undermines the uniqueness of Jesus' sacrifice. To act as though grace is a license for sin undermines the whole purpose of that sacrifice (see Romans 6:1-7). What is interesting is that in either scenario, you have *people who wear the name of Jesus, but are, in fact, enemies of the cross.* There is a lesson here for us. Some enemies are outspokenly such; others are wolves in sheep's clothing; and the latter are the more dangerous by far.

What characterizes the enemies of the cross is that "their minds are on earthly things." In contrast, Paul says, "our citizenship is in heaven." Every Philippian and citizen of this Macedonian colony would have been taught to be proud of his Roman citizenship, a privilege enjoyed by few outside of Rome itself. But what Paul wanted the Christians to realize was that they had a much greater citizenship and a much higher calling. In this world, disciples are but resident aliens. Our real home country is heaven, and our loyalty is to the King who reigns there.

In 48 B.C. Julius Caesar was decreed to be "the savior of all mankind" and from that time on the emperors were called "saviors."[1] But there is only one Savior and that is King Jesus, who has everything under his control. When the time is right he will break back into this world and use his sovereign power to transform our "lowly bodies" so that they will be the same as his "glorious body."[2] With such a hope, how can we say anything, but "to live is Christ and to die is gain"? ▊

[1] Martin, 162.
[2] **AMEN!!**

INTO YOUR LIFE

How do you feel about following the example of another person? How does your attitude line up with Paul's statement in verse 17?

Where do you see enemies of the cross today? In Paul's day they were *in* religion as well as outside of religion. Do you see them in both places today?

What is the danger of downplaying the reality of enemies?

What does "our citizenship is in heaven" mean to you? Why is a citizen of heaven going to have enemies in this world?

PERSONAL DECISION:

1 F OTHER PEOPLE'S SPIRITUAL GROWTH IS NOT OUR CONCERN, IT WILL NEVER BE OUR JOY. IF OTHERS ARE NOT OUR JOY IN THIS LIFE, THEY WILL NEVER BECOME OUR CROWN AFTER THIS LIFE.

23

MY JOY AND CROWN

Therefore, my brothers, whom I love and long for, my joy and crown, that is how you should stand firm in the Lord, dear friends! (Philippians 4:1).

When Paul died, what would he leave behind to show the worth of his life? Plaques on the wall? Induction into the Pharisee Hall of Fame? A eulogy by a high-ranking government official? No. The importance and impact of his life would be measured in other ways. For the Greeks, the crown was a symbol of victory in a contest or a token of honor bestowed on someone of high merit. Paul's crown, his victory, would be proclaimed by the changed lives of the people for whom he daily lived his life. His legacy would be lasting; his reward would be eternal. To the Corinthian disciples Paul wrote,

You yourselves are our letter, written on our hearts, known and read by everybody. You show that you are a letter from Christ, the result of our ministry, written not with ink but with the Spirit of the living God, not on tablets of stone but on the tablets of human hearts (2 Corinthians 3:2-3).

What a powerful image! Faithful disciples were a special letter written by Christ himself—a letter that gave Paul the divine recommendation that validated his life and "the result of his ministry." These disciples, who had turned from worthless idols, showed the worth of one man's life and sacrifice. Obedient disciples were his joy; therefore, they became his crown.

The Joy of Christ
If other people's spiritual growth is not our concern, it will never be our joy. If others are not our joy *in* this life, they will

never become our crown *after* this life. People will only become our joy if we take on God's heart toward them. We can fake service; we can fake devotion, but we can never fake inner joy. In the shadow of the cross, Jesus prayed that his followers would "have the full measure of [his] joy within them" (John 17:13). That joy comes to us only as we daily make our Gethsemane decision and lay down our lives for others to grow close to the Father. No matter what comes and goes, no matter *who* comes and goes, there will always be people who are faithful to God. They are gifts from God that give us a reason for joy.

We see over and over that Paul took on the mind and attitudes of Christ. What brought Jesus joy brought Paul joy. This is a checkpoint of our Christianity—where do we get our joy in this life? Is it dependent upon circumstances? Upon life being painless? Upon people acting the way they should? Upon God acting the way we think he should?

Self-centeredness is the greatest roadblock to joy. We cannot be concerned about the things of God if our own things consume our hearts and minds. And true joy will elude us if we are not concerned about the things of God. We can pout about not having joy, or, like Paul, we can give ourselves to others and discover that joy quietly sneaks into our hearts when we are looking the other way—that is, when we are looking outward instead of inward.

Because of his commitment to these brothers and sisters, these "dear friends," Paul taught them how to "stand firm in the Lord." His joy was to see their continued growth and progress. He was open with his life and his struggles. He shared his own determination to press on toward the goal, and he called them to follow his example and to think spiritually about all things. He lived and taught the message that would enable them to stay faithful. And he always reminded them that it was only through God's power that he and they would win the final victory.

These disciples were his concern and his focus. Therefore, they were his joy and his crown. ⟫

INTO
YOUR
LIFE

Think of the people who are your letter of recommendation from Christ, the ones you have helped to grow. Write down some of their names and think of their faces.

Now think of non-disciples you want to influence for Jesus. Are there specific people who quickly come to mind? If not, pray for God to bring someone to your mind or into your life. We will affect people only if we are personally concerned about them and committed to them.

How do you want to grow in your concern for others' spiritual growth, and thus in others becoming your joy?

What victory or honor are you seeking in your day-to-day life? Is it something you can put into the bank or hang on your wall? Is it the approval of others or the approval of God?

Where do you get your joy in this life? To what extent is self-centeredness a roadblock to your joy?

PERSONAL DECISION:

EVEN MATURE
DISCIPLES NEED
CHALLENGE AND HELP
TO DEAL WITH THEIR
HEARTS AND MAINTAIN
UNITY.

24

WORK IT OUT!

I plead with Euodia and I plead with Syntyche to agree with each other in the Lord. Yes, and I ask you, loyal yokefellow, help these women who have contended at my side in the cause of the gospel, along with Clement and the rest of my fellow workers, whose names are in the book of life (Philippians 4:2-3).

"Work it out!" sang the Beatles in their '60s hit, "Twist and Shout." "Work it out!" shouts the high-energy fitness trainer. "Work it out!" says Paul in so many words to two special friends. Whatever the conflict, whatever the disagreement, "Work it out!"

Euodia and Syntyche had worked side by side with Paul and with each other to make disciples of Jesus. Undoubtedly they had rejoiced together to see many lives changed. They had together weathered trials, uncertainties and persecution. But something had happened to destroy their unity. Paul does not simply *hope* they will work it out; he does not *suggest* that they work it out. He *pleads* with each of them to take the first step toward reconciliation, toward the cross of Jesus.

Whatever the conflict, Paul saw the disunity as damaging not only to these two sisters, but to the whole church as well. He did not send a note to be handed to each of them to read in the privacy of her own home. He wrote this plea in a letter to be read to the whole assembly! All eyes must have been riveted upon these two women as the sentence began, "I plead with Euodia and I plead with Syntyche..." No small matter is the unity between and among disciples in the body of Jesus. Paul literally told them, "Be of the same mind." Surely he had this situation on his heart as he wrote earlier portions of his letter: "...make my joy complete by being like-minded, having the same love, being one in spirit and purpose"; "in humility considering others better than yourselves"; "your attitude (*mind*) should be the same as that of Christ Jesus."

Humility Is Always Right

What a test for the hearts of these two women! They knew what was right. They had worked with Paul and had learned the message of the cross from his lips and from his life. They knew that humility and unity were essential qualities in the lives of disciples. But, as all of us do from time to time, they had come to a hump in the road that seemed too big to go beyond. Feelings, no doubt, were hurt on both sides. Walls had been built by both hands. Otherwise, Paul would have appealed to the one who had been unwilling to reconcile.

Paul did not ask for an investigation as to who was more right or who was more wrong. He simply wanted these two disciples to humble their hearts and set their sights on unity. To this end, he called upon a loyal and trusted brother to help them reconcile. Even mature disciples need challenge and help to deal with their hearts and maintain unity. He knew that if they continued as they were, their hearts would harden, and they would eventually fall away from the truth as each justified her position. Because of their high profile and longevity as disciples, they could polarize and divide the church as people sided with one or the other. Overtly or covertly, unity would be undermined.

In his plea, Paul echoed the prayer of Jesus, "May they be brought to complete unity to let the world know that you sent me and have loved them even as you have loved me" (John 17:23). Unity within the body has a major impact on other people becoming disciples. How selfish it is for the *saved* to hold on to personal differences and hurts, knowing that in so doing they keep others from being saved. Paul had good reason to publicly plead with these two sisters whom he loved, "Agree with each other in the Lord." ⑤

INTO YOUR LIFE

What is your track record in working out differences with other disciples?

Are you known as one who settles matters quickly?

What is your greatest fear in initiating reconciliation with someone?

Is there someone you need to forgive? To be reconciled with? To clear the air with? To be honest with? To confront with sin? When will you go to them? Write it down and ask someone to hold you to it.

Are you willing to be a "loyal yokefellow" and get involved in helping others reconcile? Do you know of a relationship between disciples where reconciliation and/or honest communication is needed? Will you take the initiative to help them? When?

PERSONAL DECISION:

QUITE SIMPLY, PAUL IS CALLING US TO REJOICE—TO ALWAYS HAVE A GREAT ATTITUDE, AN ATTITUDE THAT OVERCOMES COMPLAINING, SELF-PITY AND EXCUSES.

25

REJOICE ALWAYS

Rejoice in the Lord always. I will say it again: Rejoice! Let your gentleness be evident to all. The Lord is near (Philippians 4:4-5).

It is rather amazing the way circumstances can enhance credibility. It would be one thing to hear "rejoice always" from someone living in plenty, comfort and great health. It is a different thing altogether to hear it from someone living in circumstances which would test and challenge us all. At the time of this writing Paul was not in good circumstances. He had been in worse ones, but Roman imprisonment was no picnic, and if conditions on the inside weren't so good, neither were some of those on the "outside," where the church was not always being what God wanted her to be. And yet, Paul insisted that he and others could still rejoice. They could still affirm life, or, more accurately, *they could still affirm God.*

There is something about being "in the Lord" that gives disciples a reason to rejoice even if they are hungry, even if they are in pain, even if they are isolated, even if they are persecuted. Yes, even if they are marching to their execution. Those problems are not the source of some perverse type of joy. They are just what they appear to be. They are trials—hard and unpleasant things to endure. But if one is "in the Lord," there is always something bigger than those things, something more influential than those things, something that will eventually swallow up those things in victory.

The Lord Is Near

Paul knew as well as anyone alive that life can be hard. But he also had a deep conviction that whatever is going on, one thing is always true for those committed to God: *The Lord is near.* This is why the man or woman of God can be joyful *and gentle* in the most stressful of times. God is there monitoring the pain, making sure that we don't get more than we can bear, giving his strength in whatever mysterious way he chooses and working for the ultimate good of all those who love him.

> *The LORD is near to all who call on him,*
>   *to all who call on him in truth* (Psalm 145:18).

We can cry out, "Be not far from me, O God; come quickly, O my God, to help me" (Psalm 71:12) and he says, "I am bringing my righteousness near, it is not far away; and my salvation will not be delayed" (Isaiah 46:13).

What happened this week or this month? Did you lose your job? *The Lord is near.* Did someone you love leave the kingdom? *The Lord is near.* Did you do the very thing you didn't want to do and hurt the very people you didn't want to hurt? *The Lord is near.* Did the church not grow as much as you had hoped? *The Lord is near.* Did you get some bad news about your health? *The Lord is near.* Are there some things going on in your mind that you don't understand? *The Lord is near.* He is not far away. He has not abandoned your cause. He is not blind to your need or deaf to your call. He is not through with what he started. More work on your behalf is on his schedule. And the amazing thing is that he may use your trying circumstances to enhance your credibility, so that when you talk about finding life, people will really listen.

This passage is actually an exhortation. Paul is calling on the church to do something. Quite simply, he is calling on them, and us, to rejoice: *to always have a great attitude,* an attitude that overcomes complaining, self-pity and excuses. We are not indifferent to the bad that is in our world. As Christians we realize its seriousness more than anyone. But we refuse to believe that evil will win. We rejoice always, believing that our strong and mighty God is always near. ∎

INTO YOUR LIFE

Some people are more naturally joyful than others. On the natural "joy scale" with 1 being dour and 10 being most joyful, where are you naturally?

What is the significance of this information? Does it really matter? Why is being "in the Lord" far more important than what you are naturally?

How much joy would others say they see in your life? Are they impressed with the way your joy seems to shine even more when times are hard?

Why would Paul's words here lead to the conclusion that "You can choose your mood"?

How joyful do you really want to be? Are you holding on to anything (pride, sophistication, a "right" to complain, etc.) that keeps you from being joyful always? When and how will you let go?

PERSONAL DECISION:

Peace never comes without surrender. And surrender never comes without a decision to trust... How challenging to turn everything over to God. And yet, how foolish not to.

26

ANXIOUS ABOUT NOTHING

Do not be anxious about anything, but in everything, by prayer and petition, with thanksgiving, present your requests to God. And the peace of God, which transcends all understanding, will guard your hearts and your minds in Christ Jesus (Philippians 4:6-7).

Life has a leveling influence. It hits all of us. Just as surely as rain falls steadily and unselectively on everything, so life brings its challenges to everyone. Christians are not exempt. They are not endowed with privileges or freedoms that keep them from experiencing life in all its facets.

This group in Philippi who received Paul's letter were people, and therefore, they dealt with life and its happenings—good and bad. To them Paul writes two sentences that are incredibly comforting and incredibly challenging at the same time. A challenge within a comfort; a comfort within a challenge. He urges them not to be anxious and worried about anything, and he tells them to pray about everything because God is in control—a tall order and a huge promise rolled into one package.

Persecution. Sickness. Difficult relationships. False teachers. The Philippians had plenty they could have worried about. But disciples can rise above the knocks and whams of life. They can overcome anxiety through a powerful connection with the God who never has his sovereign power threatened, even for a moment. They can have a peace that "transcends" or rises above all human efforts to understand what is going on and how it is going to work out. But peace never comes without surrender. And surrender never comes without a decision to trust.

Being Real but Not Anxious

In an effort not to be anxious, we can simply block our thinking and our emotions. This avoidance pattern is as old as humanity itself, beginning with Adam and Eve as they tried to hide from God and from themselves. In Paul's day some Stoics sought to remove anxiety from their lives by carefully schooling themselves not to care about anything or anybody. They didn't have to worry about what would happen to others or themselves, because they did not care. If you do not care or feel any emotion, then you do not have to deal with the discomfort of anxiety. Plenty of blah, but no anxiety!

Paul's message is vastly different from that of the Stoics. As disciples we must be realists. We must be in touch with our circumstances and our thoughts. We must care about what happens to others and to ourselves. But in opening the door to honesty and caring, we can also allow anxiety to enter our hearts. Apart from the indwelling of the Spirit of God, to be real though not anxious is emotionally difficult, if not impossible. That's why we must consistently and unashamedly pray about all aspects of our lives—our fears, our hurts, our hopes, our failures, our confusion, our inadequacies. When we surrender all these to the Father, we do experience the "peace that transcends all understanding." This is not a mystical experience reserved for the few who are born spiritually endowed. It is a normal experience reserved for the ones who will decide to trust God in every situation.

The Greek word for "guard" denotes a garrison of soldiers surrounding and protecting someone or something from the enemy. We could think in terms of a garrison of angels surrounding and protecting our hearts and minds (literally *thoughts*) from Satan—the enemy who wants us to trust ourselves and to doubt our God. We can be secure in knowing that we are not on our own when difficult times come our way. Our natural impulse may be to trust and believe any fearful, panicky thought that comes into our heads. But we can trust God to guard our thinking, to give us his perspective. Our own thoughts are not always truth, but his *are* always truth. And he will never leave us.

How challenging to turn everything over to God. And yet, how foolish not to! ⑊

INTO
YOUR
LIFE

How recently have you been in a situation when you wondered where God was or if he cared? What conviction does this passage give you about trusting God?

In what ways are you stoic (blocking or ignoring your feelings) in dealing with your challenges? Why do you do this? How will you change it?

When your thoughts are not thoughts of faith, how do you fight to think faithfully? How do you test your thinking before you believe it?

Paul puts the highest priority on prayer and petition to God. Do you? The consistency and intensity of your times with God reflect your true conviction about the power of prayer. How consistent and intense are you?

What changes do you need to make in your prayer life? Get real and get specific. Do you really believe you can make these changes with God's help?

PERSONAL DECISION:

RIGHT THINKING FOCUSED ON THE TRUTH OF GOD WILL KEEP CHRISTIANS DOING THE WILL OF GOD WHATEVER IS GOING ON CIRCUMSTANTIALLY OR EMOTIONALLY.

27

MIND CHANGE

Finally, brothers, whatever is true, whatever is noble, whatever is right, whatever is pure, whatever is lovely, whatever is admirable—if anything is excellent or praiseworthy—think about such things. Whatever you have learned or received or heard from me, or seen in me—put it into practice. And the God of peace will be with you (Philippians 4:8-9).

What kind of day did you have yesterday? What kind of week have you had? In what direction is your thinking tending to go? Are you feeling positive and upbeat or negative and discouraged? Ready to take on the world or head back to bed? Paul's message to you is this: When you are "in the Lord" (back to verse 4), you can always change your mind, and when you change your mind, everything changes. If life is feeling like a heavy weight, if problems are threatening to overwhelm you, if the forecast offers little hope of sunshine, you can still set your mind on right and good things that will change the way you feel.

There are things that are *true*: God is for real. He is in control. Jesus came out of that tomb. Your sins have been forgiven. The end is going to be great.

There are things that are *noble*: Qualities of high moral character—courage, perseverance, generosity and honor. They count.

There are things that are *right* and *pure*: Patience, kindness and compassion. Confession, tears of forgiveness, tears of joy.

There are things that are *lovely* and *admirable*: The star-filled heavens on a moonless night. A sunrise. A sunset. A flock of geese. The intimacy of marriage, the special bond between parent and child, the friendship of those who have fellowship in Christ. A new disciple coming up out of the water of baptism, smiling and forgiven.

There are things that are *excellent* and *praiseworthy*: The wonders of the creation—the intricacies of the universe, the mysteries of nature. The wonder of the incarnation—God on earth, touching, healing, giving hope, giving his all. The wonders of the new creation—self-sacrifice in a selfish world, faith in the face of hardships, love in the midst of hate.

You Have a Choice

"What A Mess!" read the cover of a popular news magazine the week this article was written. The story was about a famous trial whose main characters became ubiquitous on TV screens throughout the world. But that phrase describes the way life around us can often be. And when it is that way, you have a choice: You can focus on the mess or you can change your mind and focus on who God is, what God can do, the qualities he can put in our lives, the changes he can make, the victory he will most certainly achieve, and the grace that will allow you to share in it.

The Bible's writers are not hopeful about the world's prospects. On this earth things will not get permanently better. When Jesus looks ahead, he sees "the increase of wickedness" (Matthew 24:12) not a great new world order. But while pessimistic about the world's chances, the Bible is totally optimistic about the future of God, the security of the kingdom and the plan for his people. When we set our minds on these things, we can rejoice even though the world is a mess, even though our circumstances are challenging, and even though our dreams haven't yet come true.

Will such right thinking anesthetize us? Will it lift us up above the pain so that we will feel none of it? Not at all. Disciples of Jesus aren't going to escape pain. That was never in the plan. But right thinking focused on the truth of God will keep Christians doing the will of God whatever is going on circumstantially or emotionally. Jesus summarized it: "In this world you will have trouble. But take heart! I have overcome the world" (John 16:33). ∎

INTO
YOUR
LIFE

Are you naturally more optimistic or pessimistic? How do your moods affect your outlook?

How does Paul's challenge here help us to take control of our moods and emotions?

How in touch are you with the way you think? How much conscious effort have you put into changing the way you think?

What changes in your thinking do you want to make, starting today?

Take each category Paul mentions and list other specific things on which you need to focus your mind.

PERSONAL DECISION:

117

The secret? "I can do all things through him who gives me strength."

28

I HAVE LEARNED THE SECRET

I rejoice greatly in the Lord that at last you have renewed your concern for me. Indeed, you have been concerned, but you had no opportunity to show it. I am not saying this because I am in need, for I have learned to be content whatever the circumstances. I know what it is to be in need, and I know what it is to have plenty. I have learned the secret of being content in any and every situation, whether well fed or hungry, whether living in plenty or in want. I can do everything through him who gives me strength (Philippians 4:10-13).

Jesus did not come into a world that was a blank slate. The early Christians did not practice their faith in a vacuum. Hundreds of years of religion and culture preceded the entrance of God's ultimate solution. In Philippi people were practicing their own religions and teaching their own philosophies. Many in this military colony would, no doubt, have been associated with the "mystery religions" or the "mystery cults." The skepticism and agnosticism of the philosophers had undermined faith in the old Greek and Roman gods and these groups, with their novel and fascinating rituals, rose to meet the spiritual needs of the people. Males particularly were attracted to these forms of spirituality which usually involved dramatic and often bizarre rituals. In one popular cult the initiates were placed in a pit. A bull was then slaughtered on a grid covering the pit, and the inductees drank the blood as it dripped below. The term "mystery religions" was used because at their initiation, cultists were told certain secrets they swore never to divulge.

We have already called attention to the prominence of the Stoic philosophy in this part of the world. As described earlier, the Stoics thought the best life was found by getting rid of all desire and all attachment to things, to animals *or to persons*. What the Stoics were most in pursuit of was "contentment." This came, they taught, when the flame of desire was completely blown out so that they did not care at all about having anything.

Same Words, New Meaning

In this situation, Paul plucks words from the beliefs of his day and gives them entirely new meanings. First he says, "I have learned to be *content* whatever the circumstances." He uses the favorite word of every Stoic—the Greek word *autarkeia*. To the Stoic it meant "self-sufficiency or not needing a thing because I have mastered myself." Paul had something else in mind.

Next he says, "I have learned the secret," he is using the very words found in the mystery religions—the literal translation being, "I have been initiated." "What those people are looking for in those groups," Paul says, "I have found. I now know the real secret to life." The secret? "I can do all things through him who gives me strength."

Paul didn't learn the secret of true contentment by disciplining his mind to say, "I don't care." He didn't have it whispered to him before he climbed into a pit to participate in a bloody ritual to prove his manhood. He learned it by listening every day to Jesus Christ and by putting into practice day after day the message of the cross. He learned it by holding on to his faith in the fiery trials. He says he *learned* it. Is there any reason to doubt that he learned it the old-fashioned way—slowly and sometimes painfully?

Paul did not rise from baptism having all this perfectly in place, but he did come out of that water ready to learn; and year after year, he did learn. At one point, bad circumstances led him to despair of even life itself (2 Corinthians 1:8)—he was hardly the picture of contentment. But he did not quit, and he learned from it, and he persevered through such experiences, gaining a deeper understanding from each one that God would always be faithful in every situation. ∎

INTO
YOUR
LIFE

Why do you think Paul drew on the language of other groups to make his point to the Philippians?

What "language" do you hear from others today who are trying to find life? How can you use the language of the Bible and of Jesus Christ to give them the answers they are seeking?

How can you learn from experiences that God is always faithful and always enough?

What circumstances are in your life right now that could lead to a lack of "contentment"? How can you apply the message of this passage to your situation?

PERSONAL DECISION:

GOD'S RESOURCES ENCOUNTER NO BARRICADES. HIS RICHES CANNOT BE IMPOUNDED. NO MATTER OUR SITUATION, GOD CAN CONNECT US WITH WHATEVER WE NEED.

29

MY GOD WILL MEET YOUR NEEDS

Yet it was good of you to share in my troubles. Moreover, as you Philippians know, in the early days of your acquaintance with the gospel, when I set out from Macedonia, not one church shared with me in the matter of giving and receiving, except you only; for even when I was in Thessalonica, you sent me aid again and again when I was in need. Not that I am looking for a gift, but I am looking for what may be credited to your account. I have received full payment and even more; I am amply supplied, now that I have received from Epaphroditus the gifts you sent. They are a fragrant offering, an acceptable sacrifice, pleasing to God. And my God will meet all your needs according to his glorious riches in Christ Jesus. To our God and Father be glory for ever and ever. Amen (Philippians 4:14-20).

As an apostle, Paul had every right to expect the disciples to meet his physical needs. In speaking of elders whose work was preaching and teaching, he had told Timothy not to "muzzle the ox while it is treading out the grain" (1 Timothy 5:18). In other words, meet their *physical* needs since they are spending their time and energy meeting your *spiritual* needs. Surely the same injunction should refer to apostles. Yet, Paul was careful not to demand for himself what he demanded for others. He did not want his enemies to distort anything he said and thus malign his teaching or undermine his authority.

On the other hand, Paul was appreciative and grateful when disciples were motivated to meet his needs. It touched him when they went to great effort to encourage him and bring even small gifts to show their love and concern. His heart was warmed to see their compassion and sensitivity. As his spiritual children, they demonstrated their maturity in thinking beyond their own needs. It's the same thing a mother feels when the child she has been serving night and day for a month looks into her eyes one morning at 5:00 a.m. and smiles! She would have continued to give, even if he hadn't smiled, because she loves him. But to receive that small gift gives her immeasurable joy. As we mature in Jesus, we look to meet the needs of others more than we look to others to meet our needs.

Banking for Eternity

Paul uses financial terms to express spiritual principles. He is first eager to "credit to their account" (or affirm) their concern for his needs. He is just as eager to let them know their gift was far more than a "full payment" for the ways he had poured himself out for them. Not that Paul was expecting or demanding to be repaid, he simply wanted the disciples to see the working of an important spiritual principle: When we give to meet the needs of others, God will amply supply our own needs (with *interest*).

Sometimes we are afraid our needs won't be met—our need for love, companionship, time, money, rest, encouragement, recognition...and on and on. In our fear and faithlessness, we spend our energy ensuring our own fulfillment. In this self-focused process, spiritual joy and energy drain from our lives. We must remember that God is faithful. He is totally reliable. He has "glorious riches" and promises to meet our needs. Once we decide to believe this promise, we are set free to give to others without concern for ourselves.

Paul was a giver. He urged the churches to imitate his way of life, including his giving heart. In his giving, he trusted God would provide for him—whether through the disciples or centurions sent to guard him (Acts 27:42-44). God's resources encounter no barricades. His riches cannot be impounded. No matter our situation, God can connect us with whatever we need. The issue is not his bounty or resourcefulness. The issue is our faith. Will we trust him to meet our needs, and consume ourselves with meeting the needs of others? §

INTO YOUR LIFE

Do you appreciate the full-time leaders in your church? Have you taken the time and energy to show them in thoughtful ways? The more public people are, the more their mistakes are seen...and the more they need to be encouraged for what they *are* doing right.

Do you worry about your financial, emotional or spiritual needs being met? How does this passage teach you to deal with those worries?

Is there someone in your life who is a *taker* rather than a giver? How can you help him or her to grow in this area?

Write down several needs that you have. How committed is God to meeting every one?

How does trusting God to meet our needs guard our hearts from bitterness and resentment?

PERSONAL DECISION:

GOD CAN AC-
COMPLISH
WHATEVER HE
WANTS, ANY WAY
HE WANTS, WHEN-
EVER HE WANTS,
USING WHOMEVER
HE WANTS.

30

SAINTS IN CAESAR'S HOUSEHOLD

Greet all the saints in Christ Jesus. The brothers who are with me send greetings. All the saints send you greetings, especially those who belong to Caesar's household. The grace of the Lord Jesus Christ be with your spirit. Amen (Philippians 4:21-23).

Paul brings his letter to a close, making a low-key reference to a most amazing fact. As he shares greetings from other disciples, he offhandedly refers to the saints "who belong to Caesar's household." The Latin translation of this phrase would be *familia Caesaris*, but most scholars agree that it would not have to refer to Caesar's actual family. More likely it is a reference to the larger group of assistants and servants—both freedmen and slaves—who performed a variety of functions in the emperor's household. But whatever the specific meaning, there is something remarkable here. The faith that so unexpectedly began on a Roman cross outside the city of Jerusalem spread across provinces and seas. It moved down those famous Roman roads, jumping from village to village and from city to city. It survived beatings, riots, shipwrecks and imprisonments. And it made its way to the seat of the imperial power so that right under the nose of the emperor himself were those who said, "Jesus is Lord."

There is no more incredible story in all the world than the rise and spread of faith in Jesus Christ. It has "miracle" written all over it. From the birth of Jesus in a stable, to the choosing of 12 unlikely "world-changers," to the ignominious death on the cross, to the conversion of the most fierce of all opponents, to the infiltration of Rome itself by a prisoner of the Empire, it is the story of God working the unlikely again and again. It is a story proving that God can accomplish whatever he wants, any way he wants, whenever he wants, using whomever he wants.

Amazing Impact

Paul has been teaching us how to live in this letter. Now in this one little phrase he gives us a glimpse of the impact we will have when we live this way. Become a humble servant, go the way of the cross, be courageous in sharing your faith, keep a thankful and joyful attitude through whatever comes, and the lives of other people will be changed. The salt of the earth and the light of the world will penetrate even into the darkest and most decadent places.

Considering the behavior of the infamous Nero, Roman emperor at the time, it would not be a stretch to characterize his seat of power as Satan's throne. Certainly under his leadership there would have been an atmosphere in the imperial household that would be the antithesis of Christian truth and values. Read a little history and you can easily imagine the "soap opera" being played out there day after day. But now, in the shadow of that throne, men and women had become disciples of Jesus Christ. In that atmosphere of cynicism, unbelief, selfishness and sensuality, men and women were learning what "real living" is all about. "The grace of the Lord Jesus Christ," to which Paul refers in his final sentence, is truly "amazing grace." It touches and it transforms those who seem the most unlikely candidates.

As people reading this letter more than 1900 years after it was penned, we must not think the miracles are over. The grace that produced saints in Caesar's household can produce saints among those who work for the President or those who work for the pimps. It can change the lives of those who grew up on the streets and those who grew up in the suburbs. It can change the selfish into servants and the cynical into celebrants. Those of us who have been disciples for a while must not forget what we have, and we must not forget what it can do for others. We must rejoice in what we have and be determined to pass it on. ∎

INTO YOUR LIFE

What is the significance of the way Paul closes his letters with all these "greetings"? How do you demonstrate a desire to be warm and in touch with other disciples?

Make a list of some places in our world that would correspond to "Caesar's household." Put down some places in your own sphere of activity that might correspond to this place. Can you see the gospel going into such places? What will it take on your part for it to happen?

Write down the names of three people you know who have radically changed because of Jesus Christ. What brought these changes about?

Now write down the names of three other people you know who are not disciples, but who also could be radically changed by Jesus. What will you be doing to help that take place?

PERSONAL DECISION:

EPILOGUE

PERSONAL REFLECTIONS

Studying Philippians has given me a glimpse into the heart of God as Paul's heart mirrored it. I want mine to do the same. I want to feel his pain and his joy, whatever the cost. I want the heart of God. I desire the mind of Christ. I am determined not to quit until I have both!

Paul was not a man who competed with those who were trying to usurp his authority or position. He trusted that God would use him as he, God, saw fit. He would use him *when*, *where* and *how* he decided. Everything Paul had to give came from God. He no longer believed that his own righteousness was the source of any good or usefulness in his life. As I had to confess my pride in being edited at times by my husband during this project, I knew I needed these God-trusting, self-dying truths found in Philippians.

I was especially struck by the depth of Paul's love for people—the saved and the lost. I was called to find joy in bringing others closer to the heart of God. I realize that people will never bring me deep joy if I do not allow them *in* close enough to also bring me deep hurt. Because I tend to be sinfully independent, I needed to study Philippians and to soak in the heart and attitude of a man who had repented of his sinful independence. A man who had learned to need others while never needing them more than God. A man who had learned to offer *agape* love to friend and enemy alike.

On my own I can do none of this. On my own I can do nothing of eternal value. I desperately need a thriving, moment-by-moment relationship with Jesus Christ—one that will not change through stress, failure, disappointment, hurt or even victory. To live is to have this kind of relationship with my Savior. To live *is* Christ. **⑤**

For many years this little letter to the Philippians has been having a big impact on my life. Always one of my favorites, it is a book I need today as much as ever. I naturally possess, even in an infantile form, few of the qualities this letter exalts, and I need its powerful message to help transform my mind, my heart and my faith.

I am, like most people, naturally focused on my needs. Paul shows me in this letter that the only life worth living is the life of the servant. The depth of Jesus' servanthood is a profound challenge to me, but one that I welcome. I will never outgrow my need for those amazing lines from chapter 2.

Defending myself, looking for something to credit to my account, comparing myself to others to feel better about myself—these are all my natural tendencies. Philippians so clearly shows me that all our righteousness and all our efforts to justify ourselves is "dung." We have one hope of heaven—Jesus Christ the righteous one. Praise God that his righteousness is enough for us all.

From my early years I have naturally had an uneasy feeling about life, even an expectation that most things are going to go wrong. Paul's message has helped change me into a person who is confident that God is at work *whatever happens*, giving us reason to rejoice with gusto and enthusiasm in all kinds of situations. The battle in my mind still goes on, but powerful phrases in Philippians are now inside "guarding" my heart and mind, helping me fight and win again and again.

I am naturally one who will rest on my laurels, find satisfaction in what I have done and think I am justified in slacking off. Paul hits me right between the eyes. He deliberately "forgets" what is behind and presses on to what still needs to be done. He understood the gospel, the grace, the state of the world and the mission we have. He challenges me. He inspires me. I need this letter. Thank God for Philippians. Thank God for the Jesus so clearly presented here. ∎

Resources for Christian Growth from Illumination Publishers

Apologetics

Compelling Evidence for God and the Bible—Truth in an Age of Doubt, by Douglas Jacoby.
Field Manual for Christian Apologetics, by John M. Oakes.
Is There A God—Questions and Answers about Science and the Bible, by John M. Oakes.
Mormonism—What Do the Evidence and Testimony Reveal?, by John M. Oakes.
Reasons For Belief-A Handbook of Christian Evidence, by John M. Oakes.
That You May Believe—Reflections on Science and Jesus, by John Oakes/David Eastman.
The Resurrection: A Historical Analysis, by C. Foster Stanback.
When God Is Silent—The Problem of Human Suffering, by Douglas Jacoby.

Bible Basics

A Disciple's Handbook—Third Edition, Tom A. Jones, Editor.
A Quick Overview of the Bible, by Douglas Jacoby.
Be Still, My Soul—A Practical Guide to a Deeper Relationship with God, by Sam Laing.
From Shadow to Reality—Relationship of the Old & New Testament, by John M. Oakes.
Getting the Most from the Bible, Second Edition, by G. Steve Kinnard.
Letters to New Disciples—Practical Advice for New Followers of Jesus, by Tom A. Jones.
The Baptized Life—The Lifelong Meaning of Immersion into Christ, by Tom A. Jones.
The Lion Never Sleeps—Preparing Those You Love for Satans Attacks, by Mike Taliaferro.
The New Christian's Field Guide, Joseph Dindinger, Editor.
Thirty Days at the Foot of the Cross, Tom and Sheila Jones, Editors.

Christian Living

According to Your Faith—The Awesome Power of Belief in God, by Richard Alawaye
But What About Your Anger—A Biblical Guide to Managing Your Anger, by Lee Boger.
Caring Beyond the Margins—Understanding Homosexuality, by Guy Hammond.
Golden Rule Membership—What God Expects of Every Disciple, by John M. Oakes.
How to Defeat Temptation in Under 60 Seconds, by Guy Hammond.
Jesus and the Poor—Embracing the Ministry of Jesus, by G. Steve Kinnard.
How to Be a Missionary in Your Hometown, by Joel Nagel.
Like a Tree Planted by Streams of Water—Personal Spiritual Growth, G. Steve Kinnard.
Love One Another—Importance & Power of Christian Relationships, by Gordon Ferguson.
One Another—Transformational Relationships, by Tom A. Jones and Steve Brown.
Prepared to Answer—Restoring Truth in An Age of Relativism, by Gordon Ferguson.
Repentance—A Cosmic Shift of Mind & Heart, by Edward J. Anton.
Strong in the Grace—Reclaiming the Heart of the Gospel, by Tom A. Jones.
The Guilty Soul's Guide to Grace—Freedom in Christ, by Sam Laing.
The Power of Discipling, by Gordon Ferguson.
The Prideful Soul's Guide to Humility, by Tom A. Jones and Michael Fontenot.
The Way of the Heart—Spiritual Living in a Legalistic World, by G. Steve Kinnard.
The Way of the Heart of Jesus—Prayer, Fasting, Bible Study, by G. Steve Kinnard.
Till the Nets Are Full—An Evangelism Handbook for the 21st Century, by Douglas Jacoby.
Walking the Way of the Heart—Lessons for Spiritual Living, by G. Steve Kinnard.
Values and Habits of Spiritual Growth, by Bryan Gray.

Deeper Study

A Women's Ministry Handbook, by Jennifer Lambert and Kay McKean.
After The Storm—Hope & Healing From Ezra—Nehemiah, by Rolan Dia Monje.
Aliens and Strangers—The Life and Letters of Peter, by Brett Kreider.
Crossing the Line: Culture, Race, and Kingdom, by Michael Burns.
Daniel—Prophet to the Nations, by John M. Oakes.
Exodus—Making Israel's Journey Your Own, by Rolan Dia Monje.
Exodus—Night of Redemption, by Douglas Jacoby.
Finish Strong—The Message of Haggai, Zechariah, and Malachi, by Rolan Dia Monje.
In Remembrance of Me—Understanding the Lord's Supper, by Andrew C. Fleming.
In the Middle of It!—Tools to Help Preteen and Young Teens, by Jeff Rorabaugh.
Into the Psalms—Verses for the Heart, Music for the Soul, by Rolan Dia Monje.
King Jesus—A Survey of the Life of Jesus the Messiah, by G. Steve Kinnard.
Jesus Unequaled—An Exposition of Colossians, by G. Steve Kinnard.
Passport to the Land of Enough—Revised Edition, by Joel Nagel.
Prophets I—The Voices of Yahweh, by G. Steve Kinnard
Prophets II—The Prophets of the Assyrian Period, by G. Steve Kinnard
Prophets III—The Prophets of the Babylonian and Persion Periods, by G. Steve Kinnard.
Return to Sender—When There's Nowhere Left to Go but Home, by Guy Hammond.
Romans—The Heart Set Free, by Gordon Ferguson.
Revelation Revealed—Keys to Unlocking the Mysteries of Revelation, by Gordon Ferguson.
Spiritual Leadership for Women, Jeanie Shaw, Editor.
The Call of the Wise—An Introduction and Index of Proverbs, by G. Steve Kinnard.
The Cross of the Savior—From the Perspective of Jesus..., by Mark Templer.
The Final Act—A Biblical Look at End-Time Prophecy, by G. Steve Kinnard.
The Gospel of Matthew—The Crowning of the King, by G. Steve Kinnard.
The Letters of James, Peter, John, Jude—Life to the Full, by Douglas Jacoby.
The Lion Has Roared—An Exposition of Amos, by Douglas Jacoby.
The Seven People Who Help You to Heaven, by Sam Laing.
The Spirit—Presense & Power, Sense & Nonsense, by Douglas Jacoby.
Thrive—Using Psalms to Help You Flourish, by Douglas Jacoby.
What Happens After We Die?, by Dr. Douglas Jacoby.
World Changers—The History of the Church in the Book of Acts, by Gordon Ferguson.

Marriage and Family

Building Emotional Intimacy in Your Marriage, by Jeff and Florence Schachinger.
Faith and Finances, by Patrick Blair.
Friends & Lovers—Marriage as God Designed It, by Sam and Geri Laing.
Hot and Holy—God's Plan for Exciting Sexual Intimacy in Marriage, by Sam Laing.
Mighty Man of God—A Return to the Glory of Manhood, by Sam Laing.
Raising Awesome Kids—Being the Great Influence in Your Kids' Lives by Sam and Geri Laing.
Principle-Centered Parenting, by Douglas and Vicki Jacoby.
The Essential 8 Principles of a Growing Christian Marriage, by Sam and Geri Laing.
The Essential 8 Principles of a Strong Family, by Sam and Geri Laing.
Warrior—A Call to Every Man Everywhere, by Sam Laing.

All these and more available at www.ipibooks.com

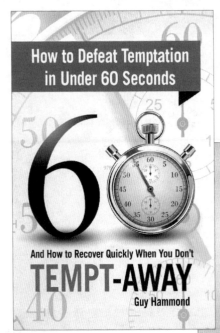

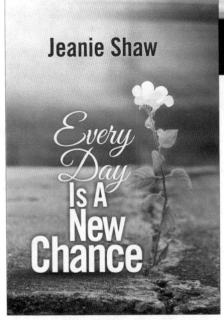

Books by Douglas Jacoby

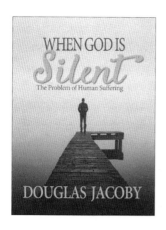

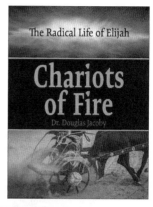

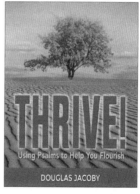

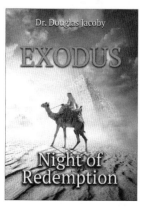

Available at www.ipibooks.com

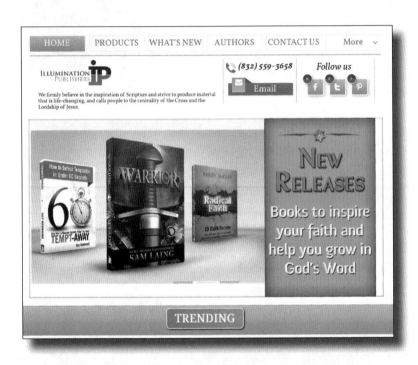

www.ipibooks.com